The Miegunyah Press

This is number one hundred and forty-nine
in the second numbered series of the
Miegunyah Volumes
made possible by the Miegunyah Fund
established by bequests under the wills
of Sir Russell and Lady Grimwade.

'Miegunyah' was the home of
Mab and Russell Grimwade
from 1911 to 1955.

Dear Sophie,

SHANNON BENNETT

28 DAYS IN PROVENCE

Best wishes.
Food and family
in the heart of France

Happy cooking,

S Bennett

THE
MIEGUNYAH
PRESS

THE MIEGUNYAH PRESS
An imprint of Melbourne University Publishing Limited
187 Grattan Street, Carlton, Victoria 3053, Australia
mup-info@unimelb.edu.au
www.mup.com.au

First published 2012

Special thanks to Izzi and Popo for supplying
beautiful props for the food photography.
Visit them at 258 Ferrars Street, South Melbourne,
or www.izziandpopo.com.au

Food photography by Simon Griffiths
Food styling by Fiona Hammond
Photography in France by Liam Bennett
Text and cover design by Trisha Garner
Typeset by Trisha Garner
Printed in China through Australian Book
Connection

National Library of Australia Cataloguing-in-
Publication entry Bennett, Shannon.

28 days in Provence: food and family in the heart
of France/Shannon Bennett.

9780522858075 (pbk.)

Bennett, Shannon.
Celebrity chefs—Biography.
Cooks—Biography.
Cooking, French—Provencal style.

641.5092

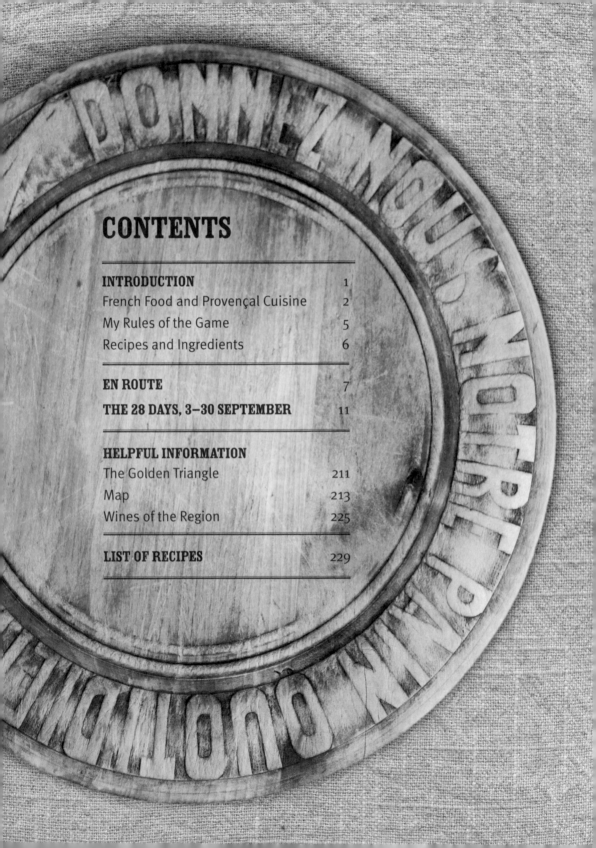

CONTENTS

INTRODUCTION

Jean Anthelme Brillat-Savarin (1755–1836) once famously said, 'Tell me what you eat, I will tell you what you are.'

Well, I know what I am, but I have no idea over the next 28 days what I'm going to eat!

With my new Vue de monde restaurant finally open in Melbourne, atop one of the city's tallest buildings, I am spending four weeks with my family in the Luberon, one of the most beautiful parts of France.

Pocketed between mountains in the western part of Provence, between the towns of Cavaillon and Manosque, the Luberon has long been seen as an idyllic place to become one with nature and a particularly French way of country living.

I have rented a large farmhouse just outside the village of Ménerbes. It is close to where British writer Peter Mayle lived when he wrote the best-selling *A Year in Provence*.

In anticipation of this month away from home, I did a small reconnoitre a year earlier while researching *Shannon Bennett's France*. I travelled the back roads, visited the famous villages of Bonnieux, Roussillon and Gordes, eating at Edouard Loubet's Michelin-starred restaurant, La Bastide de Capelongue, and at tiny auberges where the tastes of Provence literally sang from my plate.

I know these 28 days in the Luberon will be a defining time in my life, a period when Madeleine and I and our three children—Phoenix (6), Hendrix (3) and Xascha (1)—will soak in the calming, restorative balm of Southern France, and I can re-engage myself first-hand in a culinary history that has been part of my life since starting out on a restaurant career.

I worked in France as a young apprentice chef, and have been obsessed with the greatness and traditions of French cooking ever since. So, in many ways, this Luberon trip is a homecoming for me, a re-acquainting up close with so much I held to be important. Well, that was the plan. Now for the reality!

We all know that not all dreams come to pass as we wish, but France is a place that, once you let it into your heart, rarely lets you down. It embraces and caresses you in ways that will have you dreaming of returning for the rest of your life.

But why Provence? Why not write a book about Australian produce and recipes? Believe me, it's a question burning inside me and will continue to burn until I do write that book—or hopefully several books. The simple answer is that I'm not good enough at the moment. I still don't understand enough about food, culture and where Australia sits in its current identity.

My passion for food, and my selfish need for my family to believe in it in the same passionate way as I do, means that Provence draws me in. I know my answers lie within its history and way of life.

FRENCH FOOD AND PROVENÇAL CUISINE

It was Auguste Escoffier (1846–1935), the greatest and most influential chef the world has seen in the past 200 years, who said:

> When we examine the story of a nation's eating habits, describing the changing fashions of preparation and presentation and discussing the development of its cuisine throughout the ages, then we find an outline of the nation's history ...

Escoffier realized that food provides an invaluable insight into the *cœur*—the heart—of a civilization's culture.

Recent food history in Europe, say the past 500 years, really started when wild game meats were boiled in huge pots together with foraged and cultivated vegetables, or when whole wild boars were spit-roasted and served with an assorted garnish of game and fowl, or with boiled or roasted fish.

The Roman Empire introduced us to spices, wine and wheat. Then the Gauls, the local population of Provence, showed them how to cultivate grain and process it into types of flour, creating early versions of bread.

A wider choice of foods became available and more varied ways to cook them were discovered. Table manners evolved with etiquette, inevitably revealing one's origin and class.

An early example is how the Romans taught the Gauls to drink from cups instead of from human skulls and to seat themselves at rough tables instead of squatting on the ground. It would be many centuries before both Romans and Gauls learnt to eat with anything but their fingers, their teeth and a weapon, but they did place us on our modern path.

The Egyptians introduced the Romans to milk-fed pigeons, purged snails, wild oysters, foie gras made from the artificially enlarged livers of geese,

and the art of farming. The Romans then introduced these new ways of cultivation and produce to the north of Europe, establishing France's foundations for being classed as the food centre of the world.

French cuisine is extremely diverse, supported by the French passion for good food in all its forms. It can only be fully understood by walking into a local Carrefour *supermarché*. Where else in the world can a family buy milk-fed pigeons and a Grand Cru Burgundy at their local supermarket?

France's extraordinary range of different geographies and climates supports the local production of all types of ingredients. I feel compelled to understand France's long and varied history of food and culture before I can begin to understand my own.

Almost all regional influences on the cuisine of the Luberon are taken from the famous dishes from the greater Provence region we know well. Or do we? Many Provençal dishes have become popular throughout all of France and even the New World—dishes such as tapenade, pistou, *daube Provençale* and ratatouille—while many others are mainly enjoyed in the region of the Luberon known as The Golden Triangle (see p. 211). This includes the picturesque villages of Gordes, Roussillon, Bonnieux, Lacoste, Goult and Ménerbes.

The story of a dish relates not only to the *terroir* but, to an extent, a particular event. A good example is the Aussie barbecue.

I have had many traditional Aussie char-ups, but they never taste or feel the same as the ones in Mum and Dad's backyard. The same applies to being served a great big bowl of bouillabaisse in Marseille. Although most specialities from Provence are often offered throughout France, the quality and the story are never the same. Ingredients and preparation and the understanding of the recipe are always superior in their place of origin.

Each region of Provence has added in some way to the popular Provençal dishes we call 'local specialities'. For example, Lourmarin claims the *lapin à la lavande* (rabbit with lavender), while Bonnieux is well known for adding truffles to many of its winter dishes, and Roussillon for its pickled and preserved cèpes (mushrooms).

All towns within The Golden Triangle surprisingly accept seafood as part of their diet, even though the nearest port is at least 60 kilometres away to the south.

A general style of cooking and choice of ingredients connects all the towns. In Gordes, for example, the food typically features olive oil, capers, anchovies and tomatoes in pretty much every dish I have encountered, but not in a boring way. Capers are used as subtle seasoning in even local cured meats, which I find fascinating. Rosemary, thyme, lemon thyme, marjoram, sage, savoury, basil and lemon basil are definitely the herbs of Provence, but also surprisingly tarragon, chives and oregano, which feature a lot in old Provençal cookbooks but which are hard to buy unless you pre-order them. Perhaps most people grow them in their gardens.

The evolution of regional cooking has been greatly influenced by neighbouring countries and by the immigration policies of France's imperial past. France's ties to Morocco and Algeria have made it acceptable to say that preserved lemons, saffron and coriander (both the seeds and the fresh herb) are now part of regional Provençal cooking.

Every *marché paysan*—or farmers' market—I visited displayed spices and preserves that showed the influence of northern Africa. French people in Paris don't even notice this, because the Algerians and Moroccans didn't just turn up overnight. They had been trading with Europe for the past 1000 years and have inhabited the region for centuries. Their influence is simply more prominent as they have a strong tradition of maintaining the identity of their motherland better than others. This is especially evident in the Saturday market of Apt.

The areas of Provence that border Italy have incorporated some of the cuisine of their neighbour. This is not surprising when you take into account that the western part of Provence, with Nice as its capital, was part of Italy up until the mid-18th century. Also, in 1533, a Florentine princess named Catherine de Medici married Henri Duc d'Orléans, who was later to become King Henri II of France.

Catherine brought to France an entourage of Italian chefs, who introduced the locals to a variety of dishes and, most important, the tomato and courgette. These chefs showed how to integrate these fruits with fresh herbs into existing food preparation and kitchen techniques. Catherine set up elaborate and expansive kitchen gardens near to where the food was prepared in all her residences.

France and Italy have evolved into very different food cultures since that historic year, but the importance of being able to trace much of France's current food culture back to this time cannot be forgotten by anyone, especially the people of Provence.

MY RULES OF THE GAME

I will now set out the ground rules for you. All the food my family and I will be eating in the Luberon has to have been grown or raised locally, and sourced from the *marchés paysans*.

Most produce at these local markets is biodynamic. This is not something that has been advertised in the past, but biodynamic principles have been in play in this region for centuries.

Obviously, no produce can be used out of season and nothing can be processed. This means no pre-made dips or terrines. Only fresh bread is allowed and, most important, everything must be produced without the use of chemicals.

So, are we allowed to have coffee? Ah, the thought of facing a day without a fortifying cup is the stuff of nightmares! I decide that if the beans are fair-trade, biodynamic in origin, and roasted and ground locally, then it should be—has to be!—permitted.

What about sugar? Let's not get picky: all I want to do is live like a Provençal did 50 or even 100 years ago. They consumed sugar, didn't they? Did it come from the region? Of course not, but it is now part of the history of the region.

It is said that the Provençals and their land welcome all who understand it. Unfortunately, most pass through too quickly to understand much. The Luberon and its people are about the seasons, the table and a hard-work ethic that brings a quality of life not afforded to many elsewhere.

I am here to experience what provincial food was like 100 years ago and to discover why this region was, until only a couple of decades ago, classified as the birthplace of French cuisine.

But is it fair to impose this purist approach on my three young children and Madeleine, in the process getting rid of all the stealth junk food from their diets? My kids are only young, but it's now or never before I lose them to the capitalist manipulation of food for profit. If I cannot do this, then nobody can.

RECIPES AND INGREDIENTS

I didn't bring any recipes with me from Australia, so my first task is to find an old book market: I need to learn the history of local foods; I need recipes.

As for ingredients, I don't use self-raising flour, only organic baker's flour. I will only cook with French cultured butter, fresh local first-press olive oil and good sea salt.

Different salts have different flavours and different purposes, but for this book one good French salt is best and it will suit all purposes. As the best salt comes from the Atlantic coast, please forgive me for this geographic misdemeanour!

Cups, tablespoons and grams are used in the recipes. I make no apologies for a lack of continuity as many recipes are old and a few are new. Why change a recipe to appease a conscientious book editor? All I want is for the recipes to work.

If some recipes seem very simple to you, you are missing the point. The vegetables of Provence are varied. They prevail with the seasons, and when they are in season they are overflowing!

They also come with the knowledge of an artisan grower who has orchestrated their readiness not only for consumption, but for enjoyment—something even many top chefs have forgotten.

Ever boiled an aubergine in tomato juice with a little garlic and eaten it with some olive oil and freshly baked bread? Well, shush up and enjoy these recipes!

'Progress' has ruined our taste buds. We are all guilty. Vegetables have been a silent victim: swollen, tired, shrivelled and forced to submit to specialized 'hydroponics' so that shareholders can see great results in productivity! What goes around comes around.

Now, it's time for us to get on the road and discover the Luberon!

En Route

We are arguing over nothing, but right now I need to vent my frustration at someone. I'm lost and I do mean just me. All of this is my doing. Driving out of Avignon with no map and a GPS that I don't have a degree in to use, I am trying to find a house that doesn't have an address.

Why do I do this to myself? The Maldives is so much easier. All I have is a piece of paper that says:

> Take the road to Ménerbes and drive through Coustellet, then after 3 km head right until you reach the sign for a snail farm with 4 letterboxes, turn right and the house is at the top of the hill behind the farm.

The kids are cranky and Madeleine thinks I'm too ambitious, compromised by a hidden strain of lunacy that is released when I don't wake up well and am feeling the pressure.

All I care about is a long-held ambition to live a better life: simpler, with more satisfaction and purity, yet with all the luxuries I have worked so hard for. Provence offers this, particularly the Luberon.

This month-long trip is a well-researched experiment. If it works, then it will be something I will pursue when circumstances allow. I can think of nothing better than to live the rest of my life shopping daily at farmers' markets and deciding what I will cook for dinner based on what I buy that day. Let's say I'm hoping to catch the bug—the South-of-France bug.

Meanwhile, this drive is giving me a cold sweat. I've just spent the better portion of two days flying from Melbourne and then taking the TGV from Charles de Gaulle airport to Avignon.

I had told my travel agent, Frank, that I wanted the kids to experience the great pleasures of European train travel. How delusional was I? The flight had taken its toll on the poor kids, and Madeleine copped the brunt of their not sleeping for 22 hours.

So, there was no sympathy from her while I endured the living hell of the 190 minutes it took the train to reach Avignon. Reading aloud a book about Thomas the Tank Engine's adventures on Sodor Island four times in a row was the only relief I received!

Even now, every loud shout or scream from the back seat, where my 3-year-old boy sits impatiently, starts with 'The Fat Controller will not be happy.'

Finally, we find the sign that says 'Ménerbes'! With a 1973 Fiat wagon up my bum on the single-lane highway that to this day I still can't work out the speed limit of, and with no road lights at all, it's a miracle we have made it this far.

Ménerbes! I cannot contain my excitement. I relent and tell Madeleine what a great navigator she is, and how well behaved the kids have been and that they can have a treat tomorrow. I don't have any treats, but I just like getting myself into situations. Kids have just great memories, but I'm sure that whatever treat I come up with won't be good enough, anyway. This trip is all about discovery and adulation of a sense of purity, knowledge and legacy. That's the best treat anyone can give or receive.

It's a pitch-black night with not as many stars as I thought. Maybe it's a cloudy sky, but it's so dark here, apart from what looks like a castle lit up in the distance. I cannot see a snail farm sign anywhere, but I'm sure of it: those lights are our beacons. They represent a paradise island surrounded by a black hole.

Driving around in circles, I cannot find any road up to them. Madeleine then spots them: four letterboxes hidden behind an olive tree that is older than time itself. Above the tree is a sign that has a picture of a snail! We have driven past this sign at least four times. I'm an idiot.

There is no humility associated with the effects of long-distance jet travel, just a sense of covering up your mistakes without the missus knowing and trying to make the result look like I was the saviour. Anyway, if they don't like it, they should just remember: I'm cooking them more than 60 meals over the next month.

Arriving at the house, we find Collin, thin and gaunt but with a healthy stature and a Jacques Cousteau tan. He and his friend Rose usher us into the living room, where we are presented with a table full of dishes, all local recipes.

There are at least five varieties of goat's cheese, local smoked hams, a type of courgette ratatouille, local smoked trout and two amazing terrines. One is a pork-liver parfait, the other a type of *campagne*, which is a coarse mix made up of liver and meat, then baked. It has a touch of heat from a locally grown pepper.

There are also courgette flowers simply sautéed, cucumbers in a *crème farce*, local salt flakes and finely chopped chives with a local baguette and a miche (large pan loaf). Bread is one topic I am very keen to find out more about: I have read that the origin of the baguette and French bread in general lies here. Collin tells me about a bakery in the nearby village of Bonnieux that sounds particularly interesting.

After this delicious and welcoming meal, we happily collapse into our beds.

After thirty hours of travel, and jetting across the globe,
you'd think obtaining eight hours of sleep in a 300-year-old
provincial farmhouse with 90-centimetre-thick walls and
small windows blacked out beautifully with velvet curtains
would be simple. But no. I wake up with what seems like
a hangover from all the excitement at last night's arrival.
I notice in the morning light the old stone walls encasing
exposed wooden beams, and the broken slabstone pieces
dotting the floor between old-world porous grouting. This is
a wonderful house.

Downstairs the kitchen gets me really thinking: two wall-
mounted ovens, a steamer, two double fridges, a chargrill
and a walk-in wine cellar full of Côtes-du-Luberon in 1.5-litre
bottles at 9€. (This cellar would also prove invaluable for
maturing local cheeses, and storing fruit and vegetables
from the gardens.) My only criticism of the kitchen is the
Gagenau appliances. Since the company was bought out by
Bosch, I have found the quality has dropped.

The two vegetable patches flow out of the back door from the kitchen, one mainly growing gardening herbs, such as tarragon, savoury, several types of thyme, rosemary and oregano. The main vegetable patch is abundant with basil, tomatoes, celery, chillies and courgettes.

Surrounding the back of the house and outdoor pool are 500-year-old olive trees laden with green olives. The backyard faces west, so waking up before 6 am gives you an incredible aspect back towards Ménebres lighting up the chestnut trees.

Looking back at the house, it looks complex, with several external stone staircases connecting the six bedrooms with the downstairs living area. Our Luberon adventure has begun.

~

It's Saturday, so what does the local tourist website say about markets for today? Well, there is one in Oppède and that's just 2 kilometres away. Fantastic!

However, driving through the quaint—though certainly not the prettiest—town, all I see is a parked van beside a table with a few simple vegetables on it. Oh, no! I think I've had the wrong conceptions about farmers' markets in France.

I keep driving and spot a sign for Oppède-le-Vieux. This village is a further 2 kilometres up a windy road into the foothills. And half of that journey has to be made on foot, as a lovely swathe of parkland separates the town from the main thoroughfare. So, with Xascha strapped to my back, we wind our way skyward.

The town really is stunningly beautiful and rich with history. A couple of restaurants are positioned around the

Saturday, 3 September

main square, which makes it a great place to sit in the early morning or late afternoon and have a quiet, thoughtful moment. But it is all suspiciously tranquil for a market day.

After wandering around the town, the silence broken only by the occasional growling stomach, I finally approach a local café owner to enquire where the market is. 'Is not 'ere. In Apt this week.' Right, so back down the hill then.

At this point, Ménerbes seems like a good option. It's only 3 kilometres away and famed for its produce.

After successfully driving the wrong way down a number of streets and almost being poleaxed by a furniture truck, we discover that Ménerbes doesn't have a market on Saturdays. Of course!

Departing the village to the strains of Madeleine's grinding teeth, while Phoenix feigns malnutrition in the back seat, all I know is I need to find a market ... and urgently.

Avignon! It's 40 kilometres away, but at least I know I can get some fresh produce that will be local. So, with the promise of hot chocolates all round as a bribe, I drag the troops along the D900 to the Les Halles d'Avignon, which is like a small version of the Bocuse market in Lyon. It has all you need to hold one hell of a dinner party. But it is a city market, which on a Saturday equates to big crowds and major parking dramas.

After successfully hurdling both with only the odd expletive, the team rallies admirably thanks to the generous samples being pressed upon us by stallholders: succulent Cavaillon melon wedges, chunks of smooth Comté (hang on, Comté isn't from Provence), a sneaky tipple of the local rosé for Madeleine and me, and ... pain au chocolat! Suddenly,

I am a hero and the prospect of visiting markets every day doesn't seem so bad.

We pick up masses of wild garlic (for an *aigo boulido*), a whole wild rabbit (a dead giveaway that I am a chef, according to the butcher), a quarter loaf of miche, a lobe of foie gras (Madeleine threatens to throw herself on the ground and chuck a tantrum to rival Hendrix if I don't pick one up ... God help me if the kids become similarly addicted), beautiful tomatoes (coming out of the Aussie winter, it's like rediscovering an old friend), a couple of good local wines, and all the fresh fruit and vegetables we can carry.

I also duck into a small *librairie* (bookshop), where I purchase a few paperback cookbooks. None is the history of Provençal cooking that I'm looking for, but they'll have to do for now.

As we head home with the promise of some amazing meals before us, we are all sated and happy ... and the kids don't even notice I didn't get them the hot chocolates.

Herbs of Provence

VERBENA, HYSSOP, WILD THYME, BERGAMOT, SAVOURY, AGASTACHE, MARJORAM, WORMWOOD, MINT, SPEARMINT, LEMON BASIL, LEMON BALM, WILD ROCKET, POPPY FLOWERS, CROCUS, WILD WATERCRESS, WHITE CLOVER AND, OF COURSE, LAVENDER.

AIGO BOULIDO

Makes 1 litre

This Provençal soup dates back more than 300 years and uses the bare minimum of ingredients. The main unwritten rule about this recipe is its use of garlic and herbs. If made with love, this soup can be a masterpiece.

I first came across this recipe during my apprenticeship. I found the idea of a herb and garlic broth tasteless and boring. French chef Michel Bras changed my mind. His version, and trust me there are many, was beyond what food is meant to taste like. The soup, made up of wild herbs, wild garlic and water, turned Michel Bras into a storyteller. My version is inspired by Bras'.

Wild garlic and wild carrots are in abundance in Provence. The wild carrots have very thin roots and are white in colour. According to a local farmer, the smaller growers abandoned their crops many years ago and let them go to seed. But every year they now reappear.

The wild garlic is actually three-corner onion weed and I love using it back in Melbourne, so why not on my first full day here?

Madeleine has picked up some snails from our neighbours' snail farm. Phoenix is keen on keeping them as pets, but I'm keen on eating them. There is an awkward conflict here!

1 litre water

20 stems wild garlic

4 shallots, peeled and thinly sliced

10 cloves garlic

1 bunch grapes

10 bay leaves

1 teaspoon crushed coriander seeds

1 teaspoon crushed white peppercorns

2 lemons, zested and juiced

6 sprigs thyme

6 sprigs marjoram

6 sprigs tarragon

olive oil

salt to taste

Place the water, wild garlic, shallots, garlic, grapes, bay leaves, coriander seeds, peppercorns, and lemon juice and zest into a large saucepan. Bring to the boil and simmer for 1 hour.

Purée in a blender.

Whilst the stock is still very hot, return to the saucepan. Bring back to the boil and then remove from the stove. Add the herbs and rest for 5 minutes.

Place back in the blender and blend until smooth.

Pass the soup through a fine strainer. Add some olive oil and salt to taste, and serve.

I recommend serving with some garlic snails (p. 155)—provided your 6-year-old daughter will let you have them!

BRAISED WILD RABBIT WITH CARROTS, ROASTED ROSEMARY POTATOES Serves 4 and an infant

1 × 2 kg farmed rabbit

olive oil (be generous)

2 tablespoons baby capers

20 baby silver onions, peeled

salt and pepper

½ bottle dry white wine

500 ml water

8 medium home-grown carrots, with dirt still on them

8 sprigs thyme

2 bay leaves

6 large Spunta potatoes, steamed until soft

5 tablespoons chicken or goose fat

1 sprig rosemary

½ lemon (optional)

Pre-heat the oven to 160°C.

Break the rabbit down by removing the hind and front legs, and the saddle. Remove the belly (the very flat cut of meat surrounding the saddle), kidneys and liver. Reserve these in the fridge for the next day—possibly a salad (see p. 22).

Take the rib cage and, using a heavy, sharp knife, chop down along the spine to separate the right ribs from the left. This process is called 'chiming'. It leaves you with two separate rib sections.

Place some olive oil in a heavy casserole dish over a medium heat. Add the legs and the rib cage sections, then the capers and baby onions. Season generously with salt and pepper, then sauté the rabbit and onions together for 3 minutes.

Add the white wine and rapidly reduce.

Add the water and bring to the boil. Wash the carrots and add them with the thyme and bay leaves.

Place the lid on the dish and bake in the oven for 60 minutes.

Cut the potatoes into bite-size pieces. Place on a tray, season well with salt and add chicken or goose fat to the tray. Place in the oven at 180°C and cook for 45 minutes until golden and crunchy. Leave to the side and add finely chopped rosemary before serving.

Remove the casserole dish from the oven and strain the cooking liquid into a saucepan. Place the well-seasoned saddle and the other ingredients back into the casserole dish, seal with the lid and place back into the oven for 8 minutes. (If the dish is a heavy cast-iron pot, placing it back in the oven will not be necessary as the residual heat will cook the saddle very delicately in about 15 minutes.)

Reduce the cooking liquid by two-thirds into a sauce. Season once again. Adjust the balance of the sauce with a squeeze of lemon juice, if necessary. Add a little more olive oil and whisk in like you would a dressing.

Chop up the hind legs and arrange the rabbit, carrots and onions on each plate side by side next to the roast potatoes. (The rib cages will not be needed to serve 4, so leave aside for the next day's lunch, along with three of the carrots.)

Spoon sauce over the meat and vegetables, and serve.

Wine

This is a white-wine dish and you will need something with weight behind it, but also a crisp acidity. Try a Côtes-du-Ventoux–style white made from Roussanne and Viognier, the two main grape varieties in this area.

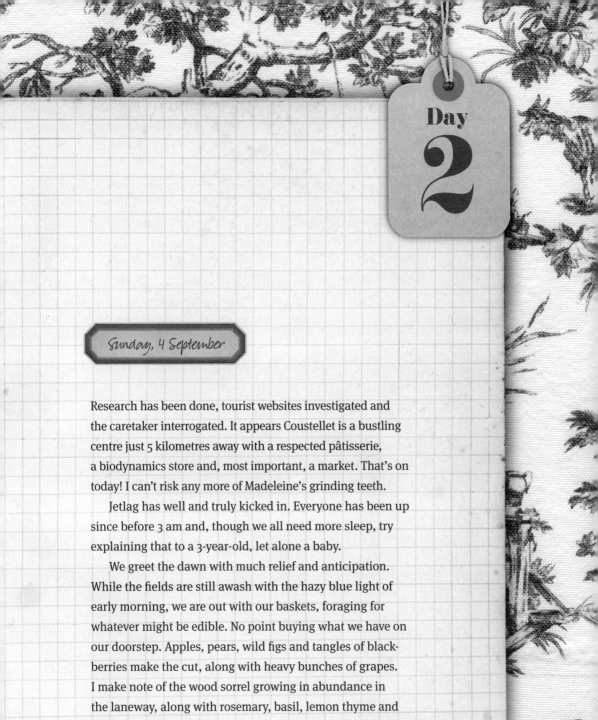

Sunday, 4 September

Research has been done, tourist websites investigated and the caretaker interrogated. It appears Coustellet is a bustling centre just 5 kilometres away with a respected pâtisserie, a biodynamics store and, most important, a market. That's on today! I can't risk any more of Madeleine's grinding teeth.

Jetlag has well and truly kicked in. Everyone has been up since before 3 am and, though we all need more sleep, try explaining that to a 3-year-old, let alone a baby.

We greet the dawn with much relief and anticipation. While the fields are still awash with the hazy blue light of early morning, we are out with our baskets, foraging for whatever might be edible. No point buying what we have on our doorstep. Apples, pears, wild figs and tangles of black-berries make the cut, along with heavy bunches of grapes. I make note of the wood sorrel growing in abundance in the laneway, along with rosemary, basil, lemon thyme and chives for future recipes.

Later, the Coustellet *marché* greets us with a heavy downpour—of course. We have been assured that it *never* rains like this at this time of year but, surprisingly, the balmy summer fall doesn't faze the troops. If anything, it heightens the market experience, sharpening the perfume of ripe fruit and freshly brewed coffee.

We make our way from stall to stall, selecting tomatoes, peaches, raspberries, local grape juice, salad leaves, garlic, acacia honey, cloudy olive oil, a wedge of Banon à la Feuille (goat's cheese) and spaghetti squash! In my days as a commis at Alain Ducasse's Louis XV restaurant in Monte Carlo, this unique squash featured frequently on the staff menu. Closely related to the pumpkin, when baked its flesh separates into fine strands that resemble spaghetti. It's the ultimate pasta for coeliacs!

As the rain becomes steadily heavier, we wind up our shopping with a demi-loaf of fine olive bread and a selection of biscuits—for the kids, maybe. The sting of cinnamon and the fragrance of almond paste make a welcome addition to their flavour, as do the chips of good dark chocolate.

Madeleine: Unfortunately, this market doesn't feature a 'disposable nappy stall' (must talk to the city council about that), so a pit stop at the local supermarket is necessary. This is one place we will be striving to avoid, but neither of us is quite prepared to drag the youngest around au naturel.

Once inside, it is utterly cavernous, like any you would find back home, and very busy with Sunday shoppers. Shannon is reassured to discover that the meat selection is modest, the fruit and vegetable aisle tiny, and that there are not many shoppers, most being here for such staples as toilet paper and cleaning products.

Sunday, 4 September

Back home, last night's leftover rabbit is shredded to make a simple salad, with the kidneys, liver and belly meat pan-fried and scattered over.

For dinner, a chicken I got from our neighbour will be roasted with potatoes in chicken fat, and the stunning tomatoes transformed into a perfect summer salad with garlic and basil.

These things take time, but everyone is happy to wait with a smooth glass of wine to hand, and the kids are over the moon at their tipple: fresh grape juice.

We invite our caretaker in for the meal and wrap up the evening with coffee, biscuits and much laughter.

RABBIT SALAD

Serves 4

rabbit trimmings
(see p. 16)

150 ml olive oil

salt and pepper

3 cooked carrots left from
previous day's recipe, sliced

10 baby silver onions,
peeled and sliced

¼ loaf bread, broken up
into large bite-size chunks

½ lemon, juiced

2 tablespoons white wine
vinegar

100 g small rocket leaves,
picked and washed

100 g curly endive lettuce,
picked and washed

¼ bunch flat parsley,
picked and washed

12 quail eggs (see below)

Pick the rib cages of all their meat (and any remaining meat from dinner the night before).

Over a medium heat, pan-fry the belly meat in some of the olive oil for 2 minutes on the first side, then 1 minute on the remaining side. Remove and rest until comfortable to touch.

Using a knife, carefully split the belly as if butterflying it. (The belly is a very flat cut of meat surrounding the saddle.) Then cut into thin julienne-like strips. Place back in the pan with a little more olive oil and fry until crispy.

Place onto some absorbent paper and keep warm.

Using the same pan and oil, fry off the well-seasoned liver and kidneys. This takes a hot pan and is a quick process.

Before removing, add the carrot and the onion. Sauté for 30 seconds. Rest on the same tray as the belly.

Add more olive oil to the pan and fry off the bread. Season with salt and remove when golden on at least one side. You want the fried bread to be both crunchy and soft.

Make a simple dressing of lemon juice, vinegar, olive oil, salt and pepper. Place into a jar and shake until emulsified, then toss through the liver, kidneys, carrot, onions, lettuce leaves and parsley in a large bowl.

To assemble the dish, add the picked meat to the bottom of each bowl.

Place the dressed ingredients over the picked meat. Lay the fried bread and belly over as a textural garnish and serve.

If you have the time and resources, I would add lightly boiled quail eggs cut in half and placed through the salad—say 3 per person.

Wine

For me, Bandol rosé was invented for such an impulsive dish as this. The Domaine Tempier rosé is a beautiful wine. The colour is an intriguing pale salmon: not really pink per se, but not orange either. It has an ever-changing aroma that epitomizes Provence, with scents of peaches and pears that evolve into a bouquet of melon and freshly squeezed citrus. The wine should always be served chilled.

How to cook and peel quail eggs

French quail eggs are nearly double the size of Australian quail eggs. They are used in salads and for stuffings.

A tip for cooking quail eggs is to drop the eggs into boiling salted water for 2½ minutes.

Remove the pot from the stove and rest for a further minute.

Place the eggs into a solution of equal parts water and vinegar for several hours, or overnight if possible. The shell will soften and you can peel it easily away.

ROAST CHICKEN FROM NEXT DOOR WITH ROASTED FENNEL

Serves 4

A simple roast free-range chicken with fennel is normally not worth a mention in a serious cookbook, but it is when it literally comes from next door. Chickens are common to this area and they have the luxury of roaming around the farms and orchards, not ever realizing their purpose in life.

4 sprigs lemon thyme

4 sprigs rosemary

1 head garlic, cut in half

1 lemon, cut in half

salt and pepper

1 large free-range or organic chicken

100 g butter

2 medium-sized bulbs of fennel

1 brown onion

olive oil

1 cup sweet vermouth

1 cup brown stock

6 courgette flowers, chopped, including the baby courgette

½ bunch tarragon, chopped

Pre-heat the oven to 180°C.

Place the thyme, rosemary, garlic, lemon, salt and pepper into the cavity of the chicken. Rub the outside of the chicken in butter, then season once again.

Cut the fennel lengthways into 6 pieces.

Peel and slice the onion into ½ cm–thick rings. Place both vegetables on the bottom of a heavy Le Creuset–type dish. Put the chicken on top of the vegetables and pour olive oil generously over the chicken. Seal the dish with a lid.

Place into the preheated oven for 45 minutes.

Remove the chicken and place on a tray in a warm area of the kitchen to rest. Remove the garlic from the cavity. Squeeze the garlic from the skins (it should still be reasonably firm) and place back into the dish with the fennel and onion.

Place the dish onto a medium heat. Add the vermouth and reduce by two-thirds. Add the stock and bring to the boil.

Add the courgettes and tarragon. Simmer for 10 minutes with the lid on. Pour any chicken juices from the resting chicken into the fennel.

Carve the chicken up into pieces by removing the legs first. If the legs are still pink, place them in the simmering sauce with the lid back on for 2–3 minutes.

Remove the breasts and carve them into a total of eight pieces. Season well.

Remove the legs and cut into 2 pieces by slicing through the joint. (Retain the carcass for making pistou tomorrow.)

Place 2 pieces of white meat onto each plate and one piece of leg meat. To the side of the plate, place the fennel. Spoon the sauce over both.

Serve with a tomato salad (below).

LOCAL TOMATO SALAD

Serves 4

2 Green Zebra tomatoes
1 Ox-heart tomato
cherry tomatoes (*cerises*)
2 yellow tomatoes
2 Black Russian tomatoes
4 cloves garlic, peeled and crushed
1 cup olive oil
salt and pepper
½ bunch basil, picked

Keep it as simple as possible. Cut the tomatoes in different ways depending on each one—quarters, slices, half slices and diced—so that the pieces are roughly similar in size.

Crush the garlic with a little of the olive oil and salt on a clean chopping board. Add to the bowl, then liberally add more seasoning and olive oil to form a simple dressing.

Add the tomatoes and coat each piece in the dressing. Rip the basil leaves and add to the salad.

Place into an appropriate serving bowl and serve.

Wine

The local AOC Ventoux from Cave Aureto hits the mark. A 2007 vintage is fresh, and vibrant red fruits explode with the essence of Provence. Wines like this are cheap and plentiful. Most are Grenache and Syrah blends, with small amounts of grape varieties thrown in to add everything from spice to earthiness. In this blend, Cinsault is added. Try to look for the most recent vintages. My only gripe is that the fruit is starting to fade, but for 10€ who cares?

POACHED WHITE 'PLATE' PEACHES IN RASPBERRIES AND CRYSTALLIZED GINGER

Serves 4

I bought these flat peaches from the market in Avignon. I could smell them before I could see them.

The aroma of a fresh white peach that is about to burst is indescribable. Think vanilla, white raspberries and a bottle of Sauternes and you are getting close.

The amazing fact about these peaches is that I can peel the skin away without any effort. It is mind-blowing produce, but Hendrix still won't eat them. I have no idea how to feed a 3-year-old boy. It is impossible.

500 g raspberries

100 g caster sugar

200 g water or sweet wine (such as a Sauternes)

1 vanilla bean, split and seeds scraped out

3 star anise

6 flat white peaches, peeled, de-stoned and cut into quarters

70 g crystallized ginger, finely diced

4 scoops vanilla-bean ice cream

Place the raspberries into a saucepan along with the caster sugar, sweet wine, vanilla bean and seeds, and star anise. Simmer for 10 minutes over a low heat.

Place the contents of the saucepan into a bar-top blender and blend on high until very smooth.

At this stage, if the Michelin inspector is coming over for dinner, strain the coulis through as fine a sieve as you can find, but, if it's just you, the missus and 3 kids who just want the ice cream anyway, then serve as is: it tastes better.

Place back into the saucepan and add the peaches and ginger. Simmer over a low heat for 2 minutes.

Place 6 quarters into each bowl and top with a perfect ball of vanilla ice cream. Serve immediately.

Monday, 5 September

I awake in the middle of the night. There are odd gurgling noises coming from the kitchen. I investigate but can't find anything.

Next morning, the rain has stopped and there is sunshine at last! The skies are crystal clear with just the odd cloud scudding across the pristine blue.

I go to the kitchen to discover what had been making all those strange nocturnal noises. One of the Cavaillon melons I bought at the Avignon market has exploded all over the bench. Ah well, I've always been an advocate for a bit of theatre in the kitchen. I make a note to myself always to eat ripe market fruit on the day of purchase!

I follow a quick, very Gallic breakfast of bacon, Beaufort, bread, coffee and a plate of fresh fruit with a jog to Ménerbes. I have to stay match-fit when there is so much cooking to undertake, and so much research (read: eating) to be done. I'm quite taken with the idea of not just being able to eat what I want, but also being healthy.

It is 3 kilometres straight up hill to the village and I arrive exhausted! At least the return leg will be easy.

Ménerbes is everything its reputation promises: quaint, historic and such a perfect representation of everything that is 'Provence'. I'm particularly taken with a couple of little restaurants I find with just three or four tables each.

Searching for a bottle of water, I discover a news agency a few doors down a laneway so narrow it wouldn't admit your average car. It has a stand-up bar and serves pastis.

To be honest, I've always hated pastis. It tastes like those horrid medicines Mum would force down my throat at the first sign of a cough or sneeze, but the romance of sitting there, in a village clinging to the hillside, overcomes my taste buds.

The jog back has its own rewards. An ancient wild fig tree beside the road offers ripe figs. One bite and my mouth fills with the taste of warm honey.

At home, the kitchen is groaning with produce from our market forays of the past two days, so I decide to improvise with what we have.

MADELEINE: A quick trip to Coustellet provides some promised DVDs for the kids, fresh milk and stock from the biodynamics store, while a bout of 'just looking' at the excellent pâtisserie naturally results in a bundle of still-warm pastries and baguettes making it home with us.

The Lion King is soon getting a workout with the girls upstairs, so I head into the garden with the number-one son in tow. We collect watercress, basil, parsley, thyme and handfuls of cherry tomatoes so ripe that they are literally bursting at the seams. Hendrix returns to the kitchen with more on his face and T-shirt than in his basket.

Madeleine is making some very unsubtle hints about wanting to tear into the foie gras and, with our second melon threatening to go the way of the first, there is nothing for it but to whip up some pan-fried foie gras for lunch in lavender honey with melon.

As for dinner, the spaghetti squash goes into the oven, and the kitchen is singing with the many-textured perfume of fresh herbs spread across the bench.

PAN-FRIED FOIE GRAS WITH LAVENDER HONEY AND MELON

Serves 4

1 × 600 g fresh foie gras lobe

1 green melon (Cavaillon)

salt and pepper

4 tablespoons lavender honey

1 bunch watercress, preferably wild

2 tablespoons fresh, chopped hazelnuts

Using a thin, sharp knife dipped in hot water, slice 1-inch-thick slices of foie gras. As a light lunch, one slice per person is sufficient.

Peel the melon, then de-seed and slice into thin slices—3 slices per person approximately, the same size as each slice of foie gras.

Heat a heavy-based fry pan over a high heat. Season the foie gras with salt and pepper. No oil is needed.

Place the slices of foie gras into the very hot pan. Remove the pan from the stove and let the slices cook. Beautiful fat will leach out and the slices will shrink.

After 90 seconds, and with one side cooked to a golden colour, carefully turn over. Place back on the stove to recharge the heat if needed. The second side will only take around 60 seconds.

Add the honey. Let the honey and rendered fat melt into each other to form a beautiful, warm dressing.

To serve, place a slice of melon onto each plate and season with a little salt. Add some cress to the side of the melon and place the liver on top. Spoon with the warm pan juices and sprinkle with chopped hazelnuts. Serve immediately.

Wine

Muscat de Beaumes-de-Venise is the perfect Provençal accompaniment to foie gras and fruit.

Serves 4

SOUP AU PISTOU WITH SPAGHETTI SQUASH

1 spaghetti squash

rock salt

1 chicken carcass (from last night's dinner)

2 litres water

1 head garlic, cut in half

½ onion

6 bay leaves

4 sprigs thyme

1 dessertspoon picked rosemary leaves

2 yellow tomatoes

2 Green Zebra tomatoes

1 large Beefsteak tomato or 1 cup ripe cherry tomatoes

1 bunch basil, picked

1 bunch parsley, washed and picked, including stems

200 ml olive oil, and extra to serve

salt and pepper

30 small baby potatoes, freshly steamed and peeled

fougasse (Provençal bread)

It's only 3 days and it's starting to catch up with me, but I'm craving fresh herbs and something soupy. Pistou is one dish that pisses me off when produced by chefs around the world because they leave out the tomatoes. They are extremely important to the dish.

So, remember the tomatoes. Then, keep it simple. If you don't have a chicken carcass for the stock, use pre-bought chicken stock.

Pre-heat the oven to 180°C.

Place the spaghetti squash in a cast-iron pot with a generous splash of olive oil and a handful of rock salt. Place the lid on top and bake for 50 minutes.

Rest the squash until required.

Place the chicken carcass into a large pot of cold water. Bring to the boil and simmer over a medium heat for 10 minutes.

Add the garlic, onion, bay leaves and thyme. Simmer for another 30 minutes.

Strain the stock and remove the carcass. Remove the garlic cloves from their skins and place the pulp back into the stock.

Add the rosemary and tomatoes to the chicken stock. Simmer for 10 minutes.

Add the remaining herbs and olive oil. Remove from the heat. Then, using either a blender or stick blender, blend the soup. Taste and adjust the seasoning.

Place some freshly steamed and peeled baby potatoes in warm bowls. Add 2–3 spoons of the flesh from the spaghetti squash to each bowl. Splash a little more olive oil over the squash and potatoes, and then a pinch of pepper and salt.

Ladle the pistou into the bowls at the table.

Serve with fresh *fougasse* and olive oil.

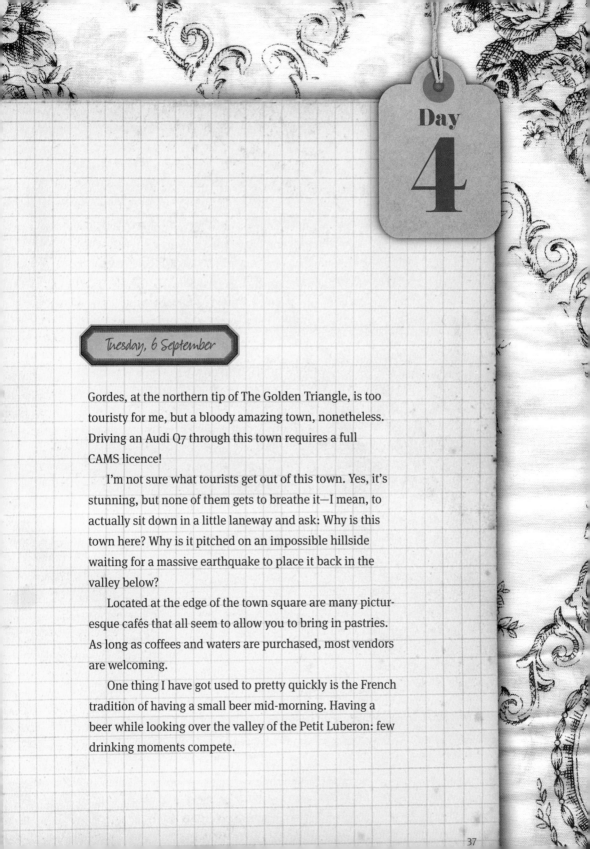

Tuesday, 6 September

Gordes, at the northern tip of The Golden Triangle, is too
touristy for me, but a bloody amazing town, nonetheless.
Driving an Audi Q7 through this town requires a full
CAMS licence!

I'm not sure what tourists get out of this town. Yes, it's
stunning, but none of them gets to breathe it—I mean, to
actually sit down in a little laneway and ask: Why is this
town here? Why is it pitched on an impossible hillside
waiting for a massive earthquake to place it back in the
valley below?

Located at the edge of the town square are many picturesque cafés that all seem to allow you to bring in pastries.
As long as coffees and waters are purchased, most vendors
are welcoming.

One thing I have got used to pretty quickly is the French
tradition of having a small beer mid-morning. Having a
beer while looking over the valley of the Petit Luberon: few
drinking moments compete.

Today is Tuesday and it's the second time I've been to the Gordes market in the past 12 months (the first was when I was researching *Shannon Bennett's France*). The *marché* is not *paysan*, which means that it's packed with tourists and sells mostly overpriced rubbish. Why would I want to buy a Gewürztraminer from Alsace in the Luberon?

I manage to find some fresh Mackerel, some plums and a few other necessities, but I am panicking a little about today's culinary delights. One good thing, though, is the little *boulangerie* (bakery) with great bread and tartlets. It's below the clock tower and well signposted.

A tiny stall selling an assortment of hot *saucisses* (sausages) on fresh baguette with basic condiments is also worth a visit. Have a beer at the one of the cafés at the end of the square next to the clock tower, and try to enjoy this town for what it is: stunning but far too full of tourists.

I also try out another small bookshop, but there's nothing to really excite me in the cooking section.

Back home, I decide lunch is going to be some roasted aubergines and Beefsteak tomatoes with garlic and olive oil on bread, plus goat's cheese and wild herbs. Dinner I'll worry about later!

TARTINES OF AUBERGINE AND OLIVE, FOIE GRAS AND SPICED APPLE, AND TOMATO, HERBS OF PROVENCE AND BANON

Serves 4

This recipe involves preparing three different tartine toppings. Begin with the roasted tomatoes and aubergine purée.

AUBERGINE PURÉE AND ROASTED TOMATOES

5 Lebanese or finger aubergines, cut in half lengthways

4 Beefsteak tomatoes, cut into wedges

1 head garlic, cut in half

1 sprig rosemary

150 ml olive oil

1 lemon, juiced

salt and pepper

TOAST

12 slices old bread, ½-cm slices (baguette preferred)

salt and pepper

¼ cup olive oil

1 clove garlic, peeled

FOIE GRAS AND APPLE TOASTS

2 tablespoons brown sugar

½ apple, peeled, cored and sliced

five-spice powder

salt and pepper

60 ml pastis

2 × 1-cm-thick slices of foie gras, cut in half again

4 slices grilled bread (see above)

For the aubergine purée and roasted tomatoes, pre-heat the oven to very hot on the 'Grill' setting.

Place the aubergines, tomatoes, garlic and rosemary in a bowl with the oil and half the lemon juice.

Season well, then lay the ingredients on a baking tray, with the aubergine flesh-side down.

Place the tray in the oven and grill for around 15 minutes.

Remove and cool until able to touch. Separate the roasted tomatoes and aubergines.

Scoop the aubergine flesh from the skins. Place the flesh into a blender with garlic (squeezed from their skins) and most of the remaining oil from the tray. Blend to a smooth purée.

Season with the remaining lemon juice, salt and pepper, then continue to blend.

Pour into a bowl.

For the toast, pre-heat the oven on 'Grill' to hot.

Place the slices of bread on an oven tray, season with salt and pepper, and liberally splash with olive oil.

Place in oven for 2–3 minutes.

Remove from the oven and immediately rub each slice of bread once over with a fresh clove of garlic. Put the large croutons to the side.

For the foie gras and apple toasts, heat a heavy fry pan over a high heat.

Add the sugar, remove from the heat and watch the sugar caramelize.

Quickly add the apple, a pinch of spice and seasoning, and then sauté (still off the heat) for 30 seconds.

Add the pastis. The pan should still be hot enough to evaporate the liquor.

Place the spiced apples onto a warm tray and put the fry pan back onto the heat.

Once hot, place the foie gras onto the pan and once again remove

the pan from the heat. Cook the foie gras until it is coloured, say around 30 seconds, then turn it over and cook on the other side. The pan will still be very hot. If it has lost its heat, simply place back on the stove.

Place a slice of cooked apple on each of the toasts, followed by the foie gras. Season and serve.

To assemble the aubergine toasts, spoon some purée onto the grilled bread and place an olive in the centre of each tartine. Serve.

To assemble the tomato toasts, place some goat's cheese on each crouton, then a basil leaf, followed by the roasted tomatoes and some of the olive oil from the roasting dish. Season and serve.

AUBERGINE TOASTS

4 tablespoons aubergine purée

4 slices grilled bread (see above)

4 green olives

TOMATO TOASTS

4 slices soft goat's cheese (Banon à la Feuille preferred)

4 slices grilled bread (see above)

4 fresh basil leaves

4 pieces oven-roasted tomato

olive oil from roasting pan

salt and pepper

PAN-FRIED STRIPED MACKEREL
WITH LEMON AND CAPERS

Serves 4

4 whole Mackerel
(not gutted, only scaled)

2 tablespoons chive batons

2 tablespoons savoury
(do not substitute
if unavailable)

2 tablespoons wild
wood sorrel

1 lemon, peeled and halved,
and the rind julienned

2 tablespoons baby capers

1 cup olive oil

50 g butter

salt and pepper

½ cup plain flour

If you are not confident with a filleting knife, ask your fishmonger to butterfly the Mackerel for you.

Using experience and skill, butterfly the Mackerel by starting from the spine of the fish and proceeding as if one were to fillet the fish until you reach the belly. Do not place the knife through the skin of the belly.

Repeat on the other side of the fish and run the knife lengthways, breaking through the bones to remove the carcass of the fish. If the fish is fresh, the stomach will be easily removed in one piece. If necessary, wash the fish.

Fill the middle of the butterflied fish with a pinch of each herb, the lemon rind, a squeeze of lemon juice, some capers, a tablespoon of the olive oil and some butter, and season well.

Fold the fillets back over to retain the whole fish shape.

Repeat for all the fish.

Pre-heat a heavy fry pan.

Place the flour on a flat plate and lightly coat the skin of the fish.

Add a tablespoon of oil to the hot pan and fry the fish on one side until crispy.

Nappé (coat) the fish with the pan juices during the cooking process. Once the fish has browned on one side, turn over and repeat the process.

Before serving, season the fish in the pan with some lemon juice and a little more salt.

Serve.

PLUM CLAFOUTIS

Serves 6–8

Pre-heat oven to 190°C.

Grease the base of the baking dish with butter and sprinkle one tablespoon of the sugar onto the base of the baking dish.

Cut the fruit in half and remove the stones. Place cut side down on the bottom of the dish.

In a blender, whiz the rest of the sugar, milk, cream, flour, vanilla and eggs for 2 minutes until all the lumps have disappeared. Pour over the fruit, which will then pop up to the top.

Sprinkle almonds all over and then bake in the oven for 50–55 minutes until golden and risen.

Remove from the oven and dust with icing sugar.

Serve with ice cream.

butter to grease

200 g caster sugar

10 plums or nectarines (or an equivalent quantity of any stone fruit, such as apricots or cherries)

2 cups milk

½ cup cream

1½ cups flour

1 teaspoon vanilla extract or paste

5 large eggs

¼ cup flaked almonds (optional)

1 tablespoon icing sugar to dust

ice cream

Wine

The 2008 Clos Ste Magdeleine Cassis Blanc, a Roussanne–Marsanne blend, has a good amount of 'oiliness'. The wine is fresh and acidic, but with a slight sweetness, which goes very well with the oiliness and sweetness of the Mackerel.

Wednesday, 7 September

For the first time we manage a sleep in. I open my eyes to the kind of brilliant sunlight that heralds a stinking hot day. The kids muddle about, dazed by too much sleep. A few vain attempts at being productive are made but soon abandoned, and we all end up lounging about on the back veranda.

Finally, I drag myself into the Coustellet *boucherie* (butcher) for some of the beef cheek I spotted on my last visit.

MADELEINE: Shannon has gone shopping again! I watch the bees making lazy circuits over the lavender, and the curious dance of a flock of wild pigeons that rhythmically rise then settle en masse in an adjacent field. The kids traipse around the property seeking adventure—or, at the very least, distraction. So, I take them for a long walk and we return with baskets full of warm, deep-red apples, their mouths full of figs and their faces smattered with blackberry juice.

Contemplating an apple, and being here, has given me a snapshot of a way of life that is so pure and whole, one I had been completely unaware of, and it saddens me to think of how much we, our children, our friends and family were missing out on. I really appreciate what Shannon is trying to achieve here.

I return an hour later as the troops are making their way back up the drive, their baskets full of apples and figs—a successful haul all round.

Madeleine is two parts inspired, but one part melancholic, and I can't get a sensible answer out of her as to why. She keeps blathering on about having an epiphany about food provenance from eating an apple.

I immediately go to check the bottle of absinthe to see how much she has drunk in my absence, but she is as sober as a wooden-spooner on Grand Final day.

As she struggles to explain her epiphany, I warn her to keep her tears away from my *daube Provençale*. This trip to the Luberon was not supposed to be a re-enactment of *Like Water for Chocolate*, but I do see her point. There is something deeply moving and inspiring about living so close to the earth, to the source of our meals, and connecting to this soil that has nourished so many generations.

There is an industrious vitality to this landscape, a constant urge towards renewal. The fields, the trees, the flocks: they all give up the fruits of their labours with a timeless generosity, which is reciprocated by farmers who treat their soil with respect, and their animals with love, bringing them to market humanely and passing them onto the customer with pride. It is this energy that gives Provence that certain quality you can't quite put your finger on, one that is sorely lacking in other produce regions.

Wednesday, 7 September

Breathing the air of these communities, you can feel the dip in vitality when you return to a place that has been over-farmed and overexposed to chemicals, where the natural order has been literally strangled out of it. You may not have even noticed the difference before.

Life here sparkles, with a subtle vibration, an undercurrent humming along that lets you know all is as it should be. You can feel it in the sunlight on your skin and the grass beneath your feet. You can smell it in the freshly turned soil and the heady perfume of lavender. And you can taste it, with every locally sourced morsel that passes your lips, especially those apples, freshly picked, still warm from the sun, crisp, white-fleshed and perfect for dessert, caramelized with puff pastry.

DAUBE PROVENÇAL

Serves 4

600 g well-trimmed beef cheek, cut into 4 × 150 g pieces

30 baby silver onions, peeled

5 cloves garlic

4 bay leaves

20 black Provençal olives, de-pipped

3 sprigs thyme

½ bottle red wine

2 tablespoons olive oil

salt and pepper

1 litre tomato broth (see recipe p. 59)

Place the beef cheek, onions, garlic, bay leaves, olives, thyme and red wine together in a bowl. Marinate in the fridge for a minimum of 1 hour and up to 48 hours.

Pre-heat an oven to 130°C.

Strain the marinated meat. Reserve the marinade liquid.

Place a heavy casserole dish over a medium heat. Add olive oil to the dish, then the cheek and season well. Caramelize on each side for about 3–4 minutes.

Add the rest of the strained marinade ingredients. Cook for a further minute.

Add the marinade liquid to the dish and reduce by a third.

Add the tomato broth and bring to the boil. Adjust the seasoning. Place the lid on the dish then put it into the oven for 3 hours.

Once cooked, the cheek will melt in the mouth. Serve with herb and mustard potatoes (below).

HERB AND MUSTARD POTATOES

Serves 4

20 small Ratte potatoes

3 tablespoons Dijon mustard

1 lemon, juiced and zested using a fine micro-plane

1 cup olive oil

1 tablespoon finely chopped tarragon leaves

salt and pepper

Steam or boil the potatoes, then peel off the skin.

Whisk the remaining ingredients in a bowl to make a dressing. Toss the potatoes in the dressing and serve warm.

CARAMELIZED APPLES IN SPICES WITH
CRISPY PUFF 'FEUILLANTINE' PASTRY *Serves 4*

200 g butter

200 g caster sugar

1 vanilla pod, halved and seeded, using seed and pod

2 star anise

1 teaspoon ground coriander

1 teaspoon mace

salt and pepper

4 apples, peeled, cored and cut in half

1 (30 cm × 30 cm) sheet puff pastry, chilled, heavily scored and 3 mm thick

200 ml crème fraîche

1 lemon, zested

1 tablespoon icing sugar

Pre-heat the oven to 180°C.

Press the butter evenly over the bottom of a heavy flat skillet or fry pan. Dust the caster sugar over the butter. Add the spices evenly over the top of the sugar, and season with salt and pepper. Place the apples flat side down.

Place the skillet on the stove on high heat for 5 minutes. A caramel will form. Do not turn the apples, but nappé the caramel over the top of the apples.

While this is happening, place the puff pastry on a heavy baking tray. Ensure the pastry is cold from the fridge. Pour off some of the caramel and brush the pastry very generously on both sides with it.

Once the remaining caramel has turned a dark brown, place the apple skillet and the pastry tray into the oven for 20 minutes or until the pastry is golden and crunchy, and the apples cooked through.

While the apples are baking, whip the crème fraîche with the lemon zest and icing sugar.

Let the pastry set for 10 minutes on a cold bench. Keep the apples warm.

Break the pastry into small flaky pieces and place 2 tablespoons into the bottom of each bowl. Place the apples on top with a generous amount of caramel.

Serve the crème fraîche with the apples.

Wine

Once again, Muscat de Beaumes-
de-Venise is the only Provençal wine
worth matching with this dessert.
But I'm not complaining.

Thursday, 8 September

Another day, another market. Today it's Roussillon.

We are up and out the door at the crack of dawn. About 15 kilometres north-west of Apt, Roussillon is more than a short drive away, but the scenery justifies the trip.

This place is considered the jewel in the Luberon crown, a hilltop village of unparalleled beauty, and I'm happy to report that it doesn't disappoint.

MADELEINE: The ochre mines surrounding Roussillon are world-famous, carved into the outlying hills to reveal a palette of dazzling earthy hues. The brilliant white, orange and red bellies of the cliff-faces stand in stark contrast to the lush, green countryside. Coupled with the strange rock formations dotted about the landscape, this creates a startling panorama, a fusion of Provençal countryside and moonscape, of chunks of Uluru unceremoniously dumped on the outskirts of a French village.

The car park fills quickly and entry to the township by wheels is not permitted beyond 9 am, so those who aren't up for the bracing walk from the lower car park had best get in early.

Arriving early has aesthetic benefits as well. The sight of the first rays of a sunny day bouncing off the colourful houses of Roussillon is one to behold. The buildings, many more than 300 years old, mirror the colours of the mines, stained from continuous extraction over the years. To see them glowing is a sight that puts the word 'picturesque' to shame. The many cats stretched out on ornamental window-sills, already basking in the gentle dawn light, delight the kids no end.

Conveniently, one of the first shops you encounter is the Roussillon pâtisserie, and it is heaven! Apart from its gorgeous period architecture, which spills out onto the little main street and throughout the village, the food is pretty good too! The obligatory croissant, pain au chocolat and escargot are matched with little quiches containing seasonal flavourings, beautiful Danishes and, a gastro-stunner, the folded, chocolate-studded brioche filled with a rum-based crème, named simply *le Suisse*. It goes down a little too easily and is bound to become a staple of our trip.

A clutch of assorted sweet biscuits follows, along with a few marzipan delights and some lavender-flavoured delicacies. Now we are ready to shop.

The market itself is small and tasteful, like the town. It winds slowly skyward, following the streets, which gather at the peak where stands the magnificent church of Saint-Michel, which affords a lovely dose of history and a 360° view of the mines.

There are not as many fruit and vegetable stalls as we would like, but the produce that is available is very, very good and surprisingly inexpensive.

I find the market to be a little disappointing. For the first time, we recognize some of the stallholders from other markets. There are only two fruit-and-vegetable stalls, neither *paysan*, and both pretty ordinary. We gather lavender and acacia honey, salad leaves, courgettes, aubergines, tiny strawberries and nectarines.

As we depart, we encounter more biscuits, this time a truly rustic assortment, much less polished than those at the pâtisserie. Cinnamon, vanilla and almond shortbreads make the cut, along with a *rocher à la noix de coco*, pistachio friandes, and a brilliant orange number of almond, citrus and honey, in honour of the famous cliffs.

As I don't have any decent protein at home, we visit the *boucherie* in Coustellet on the way back. This place is eccentric, but stocks everything you want and more. There's an excellent selection of meats, pâtés, ready meals, cheese, terrines, confiture and high-end dairy. There are also some stunning sweets and, inexplicably, many shoes of the haute couture variety!

Veal rump catches my eye. This, along with some anchovies, olives and our market vegetables, will be on the table tonight.

A magnificent *terrine de canard en croûte* with a little *confit d'oignon* on fresh baguette will also be the perfect light lunch on this sun-drenched Thursday. We will match it with a few glasses of Muscat de Domaine des Bernardins, because the butcher has a wine section ... of course!

COCKTAILS

When I return from an afternoon run, I find two pretty decent syrups on the go: lavender, and spearmint with lemon zest. Madeleine adds water to the spearmint syrup and freezes it for a refreshing granita.

Meanwhile, the lavender is blended with a variety of local spirits and mixers as Madeleine attempts to concoct a truly Provençal cocktail. Pastis, absinthe, Grand Marnier and Cognac are all recruited in various combinations, and Madeleine is soon lurching about sideways, but no 'eureka' moment arrives.

A quick email to Sebastian Rolland, mixologist at Vue de monde, produces the goods within the hour.

Try these cocktails out for a taste of late summer in the Luberon.

LAVENDER SYRUP
Serves 4

2 cups water

1 cup caster sugar

2 generous handfuls picked lavender flowers

Place all ingredients in a medium pan and simmer for 10 minutes.

Strain and set to boil to reduce by half.

Chill and serve over cake or ice cream, as a cordial with lemonade or soda water, or as a sweetener for cocktails.

THE VAUCLUSE COCKTAIL
Makes 1 cocktail

5 ml pastis

5 ml lime juice

2 pieces orange peel

40 ml Cognac

10 ml lavender syrup (see above, or you can use regular sugar)

ice

lavender stems

Provence has traditionally been a centre for perfume, lavender and pastis, but we have a problem because I hate pastis, so I really have to try to be objective here. With these three ingredients, we have made an elegant cocktail that is delicately perfumed, with flavours from the local landscape, and also powerful, for the staunch populace of towns like Marseille and the region that gave the world 'La Marseillaise'.

Using a martini shaker, stir everything with ice.

Strain into a martini or a small wine glass.

Garnish with a lavender stem.

GETAFIX FIZZ

Makes 4 drinks

Sebastian Rolland emailed me: 'For a fun lavender cocktail, we went with Asterix and Obelix's favourite friend, the Druid Getafix, who makes the mythical potion that gives Asterix his strength.' This recipe turns out to be a great drink. Garnish with a flowering lavender stem.

Put everything except the soda and lavender into a cocktail shaker. Add ice and shake it really hard!

Strain with no ice into a tall glass. Top with soda, mineral water or lemonade.

Garnish with a lavender stem.

20 ml lavender syrup (see above)

40 ml spirit of your choice, but try gin or Cognac

20 ml lemon juice

10 ml Grand Marnier or Benedictine

600 ml sparkling soda, mineral water or lemonade

lavender buds

APPLE COCKTAIL

Makes 1 drink

MADELEINE: The procession of warm days has brought the apple trees dotted about the property to their full state of sublime ripeness. Now quite plump and round, with a glossy sheen, the apples that greeted our arrival, narrow and green with just the hint of a blush, are fat and luscious, and boast a uniformly blood-red coat. The trees themselves seem exhausted, branches arching wearily all the way to the ground, which makes picking all the easier.

Of course, the choicest apples are always perched atop the highest branches, but so drunkenly ripe have the apples become that just the mere whisper of a breeze sends them tumbling to the ground. I received a mighty clunk to the noggin from a delightful sample while out foraging today, so decide to self-medicate with a soothing apple-themed aperitif.

Like all great inventions, there is no precise formula, but my second attempt based on a guestimate went down just as well.

Simply pour liqueur and wine into a wine glass with a generous helping of ice. Top with apple juice to taste.

1 tablespoon Grand Marnier

150 ml rosé wine

freshly squeezed apple juice to taste

1 large red pepper, brunoised (diced)

1 large aubergine, brunoised

1 courgette, brunoised

1 onion, brunoised

olive oil

5 cloves garlic, crushed

2 tablespoons brunoised French salami or ham

5 anchovies crushed

1 litre tomato broth (see below)

salt and pepper

CLASSIC RATATOUILLE

Serves 4

In a fry pan, fry the diced vegetables on a medium heat with a generous amount of olive oil. Add the garlic, ham and anchovies, and cook for a further 2 minutes.

Add the tomato broth and turn the heat to low. Simmer for a further

20 minutes. Taste and adjust the seasoning.

Serve warm, hot or cold.

When serving cold, a good idea is to serve the ratatouille in little pastry cases topped with a fried egg.

4 × 100 g slices of veal rump

1 tablespoon chives, finely chopped

1 tablespoon lovage, finely chopped

1 tablespoon lemon thyme, finely chopped

3 cups fresh breadcrumbs

salt and pepper

1 cup flour

3 eggs, beaten with 2 tablespoons of water

olive oil

4 fried eggs

4 anchovies, split in half lengthways

4 lemon wedges

HERB-BREADED VEAL WITH EGG AND ANCHOVY

Serves 4

Using a meat mallet or, as I do, a half empty bottle of old wine, flatten out the veal between some butcher's paper so that it doubles in size.

Mix the herbs and breadcrumbs together using a food processor and season well.

Crumb the veal by coating very lightly in flour, and dipping into

the beaten egg and then into the breadcrumbs mixed with herbs.

In a fry pan, fry the veal with a splash of olive oil over a low-to-medium heat until golden on both sides.

Put onto warm plates, then place a fried egg on top, garnished with the split anchovies in a cross pattern.

Serve the ratatouille (see below) to the side with a wedge of lemon.

TOMATO BROTH WITH BANON CROUTONS

Serves 4

I use this soup as the base for several other recipes, including the Breaded Veal with Ratatouille (above). Very ripe seasonal tomatoes are imperative.

You can serve the broth with seafood as a chilled soup or use in pastas. The ham bone plays a crucial role.

For the broth, in a large saucepan over a medium heat, add the tomatoes, garlic, shallots, aubergine, bay leaves, ham bone, rosemary and ¼ cup of olive oil. Season well and cook with the lid on, sweating the vegetables.

Add the white wine and reduce by half.

Add the stock and remaining olive oil. Simmer over a low heat for 1 hour.

Remove from the heat and remove the bacon bone.

Blend the broth using a bar-top blender. Season with salt and pepper.

For the croutons, pre-heat the oven to 180°C.

Take the ripped chunks of white bread and sauté in a fry pan with the olive oil.

Place the croutons on a baker's tray with a piece of goat's cheese on top of each bit of bread. Bake for 90 seconds.

Place the croutons into the broth, along with chive batons and baby basil leaves.

Serve either cold or hot.

TOMATO BROTH

12 large, ripe tomatoes

1 head garlic, roughly crushed

4 shallots, peeled and roughly chopped

1 aubergine, roughly chopped

4 bay leaves

1 bacon or ham bone

1 sprig rosemary

½ cup olive oil

½ bottle white wine

2 litres chicken stock

salt and pepper

BANON CROUTONS

½ loaf white bread, crusts removed and ripped into 3-cm chunks

olive oil

1 Banon à la Feuille, straight from fridge and cut into 2-cm dice

1 tablespoon chive batons

1 tablespoon baby basil leaves

TARTE TROPÉZIENNE

Makes 1 cake about 24 cm in diameter; serves approximately 6–8 people

I love to cook up a little bit of history, and this very simple brioche dessert is a great story. It also makes a simple-yet-elegant dessert for a dinner party.

The story goes like this: In the early spring of 1955, a Polish pastry chef, Alexandre Micka, opened a bakery in glamorous Saint-Tropez. He began to sell sandwiches and pizzas to the team making the film *Et Dieu … créa la femme* (*… And God Created Woman*). The cast, especially Brigitte Bardot, who was an unknown at the time but afterwards became a huge star because of the film, loved his luscious brioche-type confection that oozed a thick layer of custard. In fact, everyone on the film loved it so much that they demanded Micka give it a name. He christened it the *tarte tropézienne*, though some say Bardot actually came up with the name.

Puffed sugar is a special kind of baker's crystallized sugar used in French pastries. It may be difficult to find, but worth the effort to make your *tarte tropézienne* authentic. Try your local providores.

1 cup milk

2 vanilla beans, cut lengthwise in half and scraped

1 egg

2 egg yolks

40 g caster sugar

30 g corn flour

20 g plain flour, and extra for dusting rolling surface and flouring flan dish

1 tablespoon orange blossom water

4 tablespoons butter

½ cup ribbon-whipped cream

1 quantity olive oil brioche dough (see recipe p. 133)

1 egg yolk mixed with water, for egg wash for brioche

1 tablespoon puffed sugar

In a medium-sized saucepan, place the milk and the seeds of the vanilla beans. Bring it to the boil and turn the heat down to a low simmer.

In a bowl, whisk the egg and 2 egg yolks, caster sugar, corn flour and plain flour.

Pour in half the milk and combine using a whisk.

Place the flour and egg mixture back in the saucepan with the remaining milk. Cook over a medium-to-low heat until the milk thickens, whisking continuously.

Remove the pan from the heat and add the orange blossom water.

Place this pastry cream in a KitchenAid with the whisk attachment, and whisk until it has cooled to room temperature.

Add the butter and whisk again. Continue to whisk until it has cooled. Place it in a dish and refrigerate.

In a separate bowl, whip the cream to a 'ribbon' consistency.

When the pastry cream is cold, take it out of the fridge, whisk it gently and then fold in the ribbon-whipped cream. Refrigerate until assembly.

Pre-heat the oven to 180°C.

Butter and flour a shallow, round, 24-cm flan dish or tin.

Dust a kitchen bench with a handful of plain flour. With the help of a rolling pin or empty wine bottle, shape the brioche dough into a circle 22 cm in diameter and around 4 cm thick.

Place into the prepared flan dish or tin and cover with a clean piece of cloth. Let it rise for 30–40 minutes at room temperature.

Brush the dough with the egg wash. Sprinkle puffed sugar on top.

Bake for 25 minutes or until golden and cooked all the way through.

Let the brioche cool on a wire rack.

Place the brioche in the fridge for 10 minutes.

Remove from the fridge and cut the brioche in half horizontally. Spread the pastry cream 4 cm thick on the bottom layer. Cover with the other layer of the brioche and refrigerate until served.

Wine

Muscat de Beaumes-de-Venise goes perfectly with this tart.

The Romans were producing Muscat in this region 2000 years ago. Pliny the Elder (23–79 CE) wrote: 'Muscat has been grown for a long time in Balme [Beaumes] and makes wonderful wine.'

Pliny was right, especially when it comes from the Domaine des Bernardins, which has been producing fine wine just outside the village of Beaumes-de-Venise for five generations. It makes a great aperitif as well as a sumptuous dessert wine.

Domaine des Bernardins also make a fine red, a typically Provençal blend of Grenache (75 per cent) and Syrah (25 per cent).

FRAISES
DARAS BOIS
CAT. I
4€50
BARQ
250gr.

Friday, 9 September

Overnight, there has been a gentle shift in the weather.
While all of our mornings so far have been decidedly chilly,
blossoming into glorious sunshine by lunch, this morning is
mild and the garden isn't covered in dew.

MADELEINE: We are spoilt for choice today, with two markets
in reasonably close proximity on offer: Lourmarin and
Bonnieux. So much to see, smell and taste; so little time.
But as a wise man once said to me—he was a stallholder
selling bracelets made from shells and other bric-a-brac; he
was completely loopy, dressed like a Moroccan cult leader,
spouting philosophy and occasionally banging a gong for
no particular reason—'You have a watch, but I have time.'

I had liked the sentiment as I walked away from his stall,
forcibly extracting myself from his grasp as he tried to con
me into a 'genuine, hand-carved lute of medieval origin'
made in China. The guy might play all New Age, but he sold
like a Rottweiler.

We set out for Lourmarin. I had originally flagged the idea
of visiting both markets and, though Madeleine nodded

assent, there was a promise of teeth grinding that I didn't like. If the morning is anything to go by, the day is going to be a scorcher, and I really don't want the kids coming down with market overload only one week in. So, we decide on just one.

The drive to Lourmarin, around 25 kilometres from our base, is utterly breathtaking, the vista unfolding before us at every turn growing more and more spectacular the higher you go. This can be a danger, though, as the roads are gasp-inducingly narrow and the local drivers re-enact scenes from *The Cannonball Run* on a regular basis.

Our GPS takes us on a curly route via Bonnieux but, with nowhere to park and the thought of navigating more streets that barely accommodate one car, let alone two, we continue on.

Like most markets, the main roads into Lourmarin are closed on market day, thus requiring a short walk in. Do not attempt to bring in trolleys or prams. Just because you have to walk doesn't mean there are any paths for that purpose, and there can be some hairy moments dodging between cars parked anywhere remotely possible and the surging market traffic.

Stalls occupy both sides of the main street, and branch off along a number of laneways, winding all the way up to the relic of a medieval château. This glorious edifice actually houses one of the most impressive *caves* in the region, with a trove of good local drops and some rare finds. I buy a 2010 Domaine de Montvac Mélodine Vacqueyras Blanc, a 2010 Bastide du Claux Rouge from Sylvan Morey, a 2009 Château de Clapier Luberon Blanc and a Gelas Bas Armagnac for good measure.

Lourmarin is a veritable Mecca for arts and crafts, but for every quaint hand-painted pottery item and lacy-capped jar of confit there are two soap stalls of dubious origin, Aztec-themed flutes and charms, and even a 'revolutionary kitchen slicer' that an over-enthusiastic man behind a stall pitches at 100 kilometres an hour.

Our visit also coincides with Lourmarin's annual book fair, the extra influx of visitors straining the already narrow laneways.

More than 100 antiquarian booksellers from all over France have arrived to showcase their rare books, for this—the Journées du Livre Ancien et de la Bibliophilie—is a renowned event. Perhaps I will find the cookbook that I have been searching for.

And there it is, on an outdoor stall crowded with books about the royal families of France and forgotten novels by writers I have never heard of. It is a simple manuscript of local recipes from long, long ago, but for me manna from heaven! I can't wait to find a quiet spot in the shade to study the text, before trying out the historical recipes. But first I have some shopping to do!

Sadly, the fruit and vegetables don't live up to their bucolic setting, which is all the more sad because our visit had started so promisingly. My pulse accelerated when, at one of the first stalls we encountered, I spotted chanterelles. Good mushrooms had been one thing I couldn't wait to cook, but closer inspection revealed they were farmed.

So, I search high and low for beetroot, but to no avail. I do, however, secure more of those glorious Cavaillon melons and a bundle of strawberries that sing of summertime in the country.

The *boucherie* is adequate and the bread mediocre. But there are some magnificent cheeses, a fabulous *poulet* stall with golden chooks slowly rotating on a tiny mobile rôtisserie, and a quaint pâtisserie offering hefty slices of the traditional pissaladière of onion, anchovy and Provençal vegetables. Their *fougasse* justifies the journey, too.

We depart Lourmarin without many spoils, but tomorrow is Apt, which by all reports is the best local market. As I have already placed an order for fresh Red Mullet at the *poissonnerie* (fish shop) in Coustellet, I anticipate some fine dining to be had over the weekend.

Mum and Dad arrive tonight. Their plane to Paris was delayed, and then their train, due to mysterious 'security problems'. With the tenth anniversary of 11 September falling in two days, I'm sure all the world's capitals are experiencing similar delays.

After picking them up in Avignon—it is great to see them and have even more of our family together—we return to a simple meal of cold roast chicken, tomato and basil salad, cheese and an impressive duck parfait from the Coustellet *boucherie*.

Then, it's bed!

Friday, 9 September

TOP FIVE *BOULANGERIES* IN THE LUBERON

Pastries are the stuff of gastronomic fantasies, and each village seems to have its own specialities. Here are my favourite bakers.

COUSTELLET

Using an old-world wood oven, Coustellet's main baker is sensational. It has an incredible array of pastries on offer: sugary brioche slices, fruit flans, *tropézienne* wedges, light and buttery *fougasse* with a wild assortment of flavourings, savoury pastries and miniature cakes. Their almond croissant is, however, the highlight.

To locate the bakery, keep driving through the town away from Avignon towards Ménerbes. It is housed in a large pink building on the left, with plenty of parking available. Normally, there is a line out the door.

The other small bakery in Coustellet is no ordinary second-placer. It is on the left-hand side of the main road, driving away from Avignon, at the junction. Its breads are beautifully crafted, baked in wood-fired ovens. The *viennoiseries* are top drawer.

The other great asset of this bakery is its friendly service, and it's open on Mondays.

GORDES

Gordes' two bakeries must vie for the local dollar as they are equally magnificent, but the one beneath the clock tower offers some unique slices and flaky turnovers with a variety of ripe stone fruit, and a fabulous cakey confection known as *abricot délice*, which has thick slices of apricot smeared in preserve on a wedge of sweet sponge. There is also no doubt that this shop has the best pain au chocolat I have ever tasted. It's a big call, I know, but the execution is amazing.

The second *boulangerie*, abutting the pharmacy, has arguably the best bread in town, and wins my vote for the best croissant.

ROUSSILLON

The only bakery on the edge of the market square makes the best Suisse brioche I have ever tasted. The brioche dough is rolled thinly, then rolled into layers with couverture chocolate drops and pastry cream flavoured with Cognac. Bread and tens of varieties of house-made biscuits are also a specialty here.

Saturday, 10 September

Everyone emerges later than usual and slightly dishevelled.
I'm determined to hit the markets early today, so I usher the
troops into the car in various states of dress with just coffee
and melon in their bellies for sustenance. They will thank
me later when the midday market surge begins, the sun is at
its peak and we will be home lounging by the pool.

So, on to Apt. The town is considerably larger and more
built up than I'd expected. The market is huge. We cruise
along the river in our now-familiar search for a parking spot
that will accommodate our seven-seater Audi. On and on
the congested side streets stretch before us, but, no matter
how far we travel, an anxious glance to the right reveals the
market is still following us alongside.

The Apt *marché* is not unlike Les Halles in Avignon,
but with the feel of a genuine village market, albeit an
enormous one. Everything from the kitchen sink to the back
garden is catered for. We have become quite adept at recog-
nizing a number of the stallholders now, and they in turn
recognize us, offering a wave or swift 'Bonjour' without the
customary attempt to make a sale.

However, many of the stalls here are truly unique and often dedicated to only one or two specific items, be they tomatoes, honey or gourds. This generally suggests the product is locally sourced—always a good sign.

One stall offers heavy wheels of *pâtes de fruits*, another dried legumes, with miniscule *lentilles vertes du Puy* that go straight into the basket. Quality cheeses are available at numerous stalls, but I look out for ones where the local product dominates. I find one offering only varieties of Banon à la Feuille and bags of pearl barley. The value for money takes my breath away. The barley and two cheeses come in at under 4€!

Then I spot my first fresh quail! I buy thirteen, along with a dozen quail eggs and the same again of chicken eggs.

The sublime quality of the tomatoes here prompts another purchase. Three of the enormous Beefsteak variety will make a nice summer consommé, while a mixed box, or *mélange de tomates*, of every conceivable shape and colour will disappear into salads and snacks. How often do you reach for a tomato to eat fresh, like a peach? The irresistible colour and aroma of these little numbers are so mouth-watering that they more than justify their genus as fruit.

MADELEINE: Naturally we get lost, and Hendrix, a recent graduate of the trials of toilet training, is demanding to use the powder room at the top of his lungs. Xascha, meanwhile, again firmly strapped to my back, has dispensed with such frivolous concerns by gifting me with a large wet patch at the lumbar region. Shannon's in desperate need of a coffee and I'm faking a limp (poorly) to passively suggest I'm sick of dragging around the bulk of the purchases.

While I dart from one stall to the next, I urge everyone to buck up and get into the spirit of things, only to cop a look from Phoenix that could drop a rhino at 20 paces.

Saturday, 10 September

As much as I would like to explore further, the sun is high in the sky and it's time to trundle home. Corn on the cob, black figs and baguettes are to be our final purchases, but we are all stopped in our tracks by the aroma wafting over from a nearby stand. Enormous pots of paella, couscous and *poulet et saucisses Merguez* beckon, alongside vats of crispy *beignets de lègumes*. Juicy battered slices of aubergine and courgette put our humble potato cake to shame.

A hearty serve of everything on offer accompanies us as we set off back to the farmhouse.

I'm a little disappointed to be departing Apt with so many laneways uncharted and so many stalls undiscovered, but it makes me anticipate my return even more.

With lunch taken care of, my thoughts drift to dinner. I'm feeling celebratory and want to properly welcome Mum and Dad with a meal that is at once quintessentially Provençal but still quite refined.

Entrée will be a clear tomato consommé, while mains will comprise those juicy little quails, stuffed with foie gras, sage, almond and lemon, on sweet corn purée, and violet beans in anchovy dressing. This will be followed swiftly by poached grapes with almond milk.

We invite our caretaker to join us and, as kitchen hands, I rope in every family member capable of handling a knife without losing a digit (sorry Hendrix, Xascha ... and Dad). I've put the old man on rôtisserie duty, but plan to pull the quails off half an hour before he would proclaim them done. He is a whiz at sparking up a barbie, but is the kind of man who takes his coffee and toast the same way: black.

Madeleine has promised to whip up something spectacular by way of an aperitif, so there's every chance none of us will make dinner. I plan to get it underway nonetheless.

CLEAR TOMATO JUICE
WITH FRESH MELON BALLS AND MINT *Serves 4*

1 kg ripe tomatoes, varying varieties

5 cloves garlic, peeled and crushed

10 basil leaves

12 balls green melon

12 balls orange melon

12 Strawberry tomatoes, peeled

4 sprigs spearmint

Place all ingredients except for the melon balls, Strawberry tomatoes and spearmint in a food processor and pulse for a minute.

Season well and place the puréed ingredients into a coffee filter paper supported by a sieve or colander in a bowl. Slowly drain the juices of the ingredients.

Discard what is left in the filter paper and keep the juice chilled until ready to use.

Place the peeled tomatoes and melon balls in each bowl, pour over the chilled tomato juice, and garnish with the spearmint leaves.

Serve.

LOCAL QUAIL COOKED OVER WOOD COALS
WITH SAGE, ALMOND AND LEMON *Serves 4*

8 quail

1 lemon, juiced

2 cloves garlic, crushed

1 cup olive oil

2 tablespoons toasted flaked almonds

1 shallot, finely diced

1 tablespoon chopped tarragon

1 teaspoon chopped lemon thyme

1 tablespoon chopped sage

salt and pepper

100 g fresh breadcrumbs

100 g foie gras or chicken livers

Rinse the birds and pat dry inside and out. Remove the neck and wishbone of each quail.

Marinate the quails with the lemon juice, 1 of the crushed garlic cloves and ¾ cup of the olive oil for a minimum of 1 hour—preferably 4 hours.

Remove the quails and drain well.

In a food processor, add the almonds, remaining crushed garlic clove, diced shallot, herbs, remaining olive oil, salt and pepper, and breadcrumbs. Pulse until combined. Adjust the seasoning.

Place the stuffing inside the cavity of each bird, along with a small cube of foie gras or chicken liver.

Pre-heat the oven to 160°C, or—the preferred alternative—set up the rôtisserie on a barbecue.

Place the skewer through the centre of each bird, pushing it onto the skewer. Roast for 35 minutes, continuously basting with the marinade.

If using an oven, which I don't recommend (you need the romance of the coals and the spit), roast for 20 minutes.

VIOLET BEANS WITH ANCHOVY SAUCE   *Serves 4*

500 g of violet runner beans

8 anchovy fillets

4 cloves garlic

40 g bay capers and some of their water (brine)

1 white salad onion, chopped

1 lemon, juiced

olive oil

salt and pepper

Cook the beans in boiling salted water for 5 minutes. Drain and keep warm.

In a bar-top blender, place the anchovies, garlic, capers and onion. Blend with some of the brine from the capers to make a smooth dressing.

Combine the beans with the dressing, and add lemon juice and olive oil to taste. Season well and serve while still warm.

SWEET CORN PURÉE   *Serves 4*

4 cobs sweet corn, peeled and the corn removed

1 brown onion, finely chopped

3 cloves garlic, crushed

2 tablespoons duck fat

½ cup chicken stock

salt and pepper

Over a medium heat, in a large saucepan, sweat the sweet corn, onion and garlic in the duck fat.

After 2 minutes, add the chicken stock. Season well.

Turn the heat down to a simmer, then cook for 30 minutes.

Blend the sweet corn in a food processor until smooth.

Adjust seasoning and serve.

POACHED GRAPES WITH ALMOND MILK   *Serves 4*

Place the grapes and strawberries in the red grape juice till needed.

In a small saucepan over a medium heat, bring the ground almond, milk, vanilla pod and seeds and half of the caster sugar to the simmer. Take off the heat and leave to the side to infuse for 10 minutes.

While this is taking place, strain off the fruit (retaining the juice) and divide the fruit evenly between 4 bowls.

Place the grape juice in a saucepan on the stove and bring to the boil.

While the grape juice is heating, whisk the eggs, corn flour and the remaining caster sugar together until smooth.

Once the juice has come to the boil, add a third of the juice to the egg mixture and whisk until smooth.

Pour the thick egg mixture back into the remaining grape juice in the saucepan and whisk vigorously over a medium heat until it is smooth and has once again boiled.

Remove from the stove and spoon 2 tablespoons into each bowl.

Pour over the warm almond milk and serve immediately.

40 red grapes, peeled

20 strawberries, topped

2 cups red grape juice

200 g ground almond

2 cups milk

1 vanilla pod, halved and seeded

1 cup caster sugar

2 eggs

2 tablespoons corn flour

Wine

For dinner, we have two of the wines I bought yesterday in Lourmarin: the 2010 Domaine de Montvac Mélodine Vacqueyras Blanc (Roussanne, Clairette, Bourboulenc and Viognier) and the 2010 Bastide du Claux Malacare Rouge from Sylvan Morey (a nearly equal blend of Grenache, Carignan and Syrah). Both prove how delicious southern Rhône wines can be.

Day

9

The Sunday market of Coustellet is my favourite market of the week without a doubt. I say this because I now know the layout and there is no hiding its authenticity. The *paysan* village feel is there at every stall. Produce that has not been pulled from the ground or slaughtered in the past few days is not allowed. And nothing is perfect: no two tomatoes are the same size, no two chickens have the same colour.

I'm curious about the local lamb stall, which seems to sell a lot of hearts. It is tiny, with a small glass cabinet that contains a couple of *cuisses* (legs), one or two saddles, and the rest hearts and kidneys. I ask the young farmer what do the locals do with them? He shrugs and tells me they flavour the hearts with local herbs and garlic, then hot-smoke them using cedar wood before serving them cold with a local sauce. He could not explain what the sauce was. This made me even more curious.

I purchase a leg of lamb from him. Maybe I can do the same with a lamb leg, but serve it warm.

He also tells me that his lambs wander around his grand-father's orchard for a few weeks at this time of the year, as they don't touch the grapes or apples, and the protective mothers chase away any crows that try to eat the fruit.

Today I also discover *pimentée* pepper. It is the favourite spice of the Provençals, normally dried then ground, but I have noticed today it is fresh and in abundance at several stores. It looks very much like a Cayenne pepper, with its vivid red colour, medium size and long-and-narrow shape.

I decide to take the plunge and bite into one. It isn't hot, but the balance between the sweetness and spice makes it really appealing. The down side is the skin, which, though thin, is tough and nearly inedible. The flesh inside is also very minimal. And at 2€ a piece, it is not cheap compared to other vegetables.

I buy eight peppers. I'm not sure what I'm going to do with them, but I did notice at the pizza van this morning the owner was serving a pepper sauce on the side with all the pizzas.

They're bloody good pizzas, by the way. The locals really do get into them here. A simple basil, tomato and anchovy pizza is generously drenched in the sauce, as if to say to the Italians, 'This pizza is now French!'

PICKLED COURGETTES

Makes 6 serves

To make the pickling solution, bring the beer, sugar and vinegar to the boil.

Remove from heat and let cool to room temperature.

To pickle the courgettes, place them into the solution for 10 minutes.

Remove the courgettes from the solution and serve within an hour or so of pickling.

PICKLED COURGETTES
4 courgettes, cut into finger-size pieces

PICKLING SOLUTION
1 cup beer

1 cup sugar

1 cup white wine vinegar

PICKLED CARROTS

Makes 6 serves

Bring the solution to the boil with the garlic cloves. Remove from the heat and add the carrots.

Leave for 30 minutes and then remove the carrots from the solution.

Season well before serving.

2 cups pickling solution (see above)

3 cloves garlic, thinly sliced

2 carrots, thinly sliced

RED MULLET WITH ORANGE

Serves 6

12 fillets medium-sized
**Red Mullet, de-boned
(retain bones)**

1 cup olive oil

1 cup orange juice

1 cup carrot juice

1 cup dark chicken stock

½ lemon, juiced

salt and pepper

Red Mullet can be the most rewarding fish in the ocean. Why? Well, it's a fish that no one really wants, so it's cheap. But make sure to buy it fresh.

Eating Red Mullet is like finding an out-of-print cookbook by a 1990s 3-star chef at a garage sale. The feel-good factor translates so well, because Mullet caught that day tastes of the ocean—especially if it's of the Mediterranean subspecies.

Serve the Red Mullet as an entrée with some Pickled Courgettes or Pickled Carrots.

Pre-heat a fry pan with ¼ cup of the olive oil. Add the Red Mullet bones and fry until golden brown.

Add the chicken stock and reduce until a glaze is formed.

Add the orange and carrot juice to the pan. Reduce by half.

Strain the glaze, discarding the bones. Season with the lemon juice.

Stir in ½ cup of the remaining olive oil. Season well and leave to the side.

Clean the pan with some paper towel.

Place the pan back on the stove over a medium heat. Add 2 tablespoons of olive oil.

Season the fillets with salt on the skin side. Add to the pan, skin-side down, and turn heat to low.

Cook the fillets for 2 minutes on the skin side and 1 minute on the flesh side.

Place 2 fillets on each plate and drizzle the sauce over them. Serve.

SPIT-ROASTED LAMB LEG, HERBS OF PROVENCE, LOCAL POTATOES AND FENNEL

Serves 4

1 head garlic, peeled

1 white salad onion, peeled and roughly chopped

4 sprigs thyme

4 sprigs rosemary, picked

4 sprigs lemon thyme

6 sprigs marjoram

4 bay leaves

¼ bunch parsley

¼ bunch tarragon

1 lemon, zest and juice

1 cup olive oil

1 × 2 kg lamb leg

20 small potatoes, cooked in salted water and peeled

8 small fennel bulbs

1 cup tomato vinaigrette (see below)

salt and pepper

Place the garlic, onion, herbs, lemon zest, juice and olive oil into a blender. Blend until the oil turns a light green colour. Season the purée well with salt and pepper.

Stab the lamb leg with a small knife or roasting fork at least a dozen times on each side.

In a deep dish or tray, marinate the leg in the herb purée for at least an hour and preferably 12 hours.

When ready to roast, remove the lamb from the marinade and reserve the liquid for basting.

Place the leg on a spit and attach to the rôtisserie. Place a tray under the roast and lay the potatoes down on the tray.

Please ensure that if using the rôtisserie attachment to a barbecue, you do not turn on the actual hot plates. This will cook the leg too quickly and burn the underside of the potatoes. Also, do not drop the hood on the barbecue until the last 30 minutes or so of cooking.

Continue to baste using the reserved marinade every 15 minutes or so—preferably with a good glass of Viognier in your hand.

The roasting process will take around 2½ hours.

For the last ½ hour, add the fennel bulbs to the tray with the potatoes.

Rest the roast on the spit with the hood down for 10 minutes.

Simply serve slices of the meat with fennel and potatoes, and spoon on some tomato vinaigrette (see below).

TOMATO VINAIGRETTE

Serves 4

Using a blender, combine all the
ingredients until smooth. Taste
and adjust seasoning.

This dressing is always best
served cold.

20 cherry tomatoes

1 cup clear tomato juice
(see p. 72) or use water

2 shallots, peeled and
roughly chopped

4 cloves garlic

3 tablespoons Heinz
tomato ketchup

1 tablespoon white wine
vinegar

1 cup olive oil

salt and pepper

PIMENTÉE SAUCE

Makes approximately 400 ml

Pre-heat the oven to 180°C.

Place all the ingredients on an
oven tray and bake for 30 minutes.

Transfer everything to a food
blender and blend until smooth.

Store in the refrigerator until
required.

10 *pimentée* peppers

1 brown onion, finely diced

4 cloves garlic, peeled
and crushed

2 tablespoons small
pickled capers

2 Roma-style tomatoes

1 tablespoon shallot
vinegar (see p. 97)

1 cup olive oil

salt

Plat du Jour

NO
MORE
——
HAVE A NICE DAY

LA PAUSE

Day
10

At last, a day of rest—or, in other words, no market! I intend to take it easy, with simple meals eked out from what we have on hand. My strict adherence to the *paysan* tradition, however, means that there are no preservative-laden breads or pastries lurking in the pantry or freezer to pad out the day's dishes. So, a trip to a *boulangerie* is still on the cards.

Dad, a stickler for good bread and lots of it, declares he's up for a bit of a walk and offers to take a scenic trundle up to Ménerbes for fresh *pain*. Three hours later, Mum, by now more than a little worried, finally reaches him on his mobile.

'Oh, I had a coffee and a bit of a look around. Now I'm just having a bite of lunch.'

With a chuckle, we jump in the car. As Dad is adamant he doesn't need rescuing, we head off instead to our old faithful, Coustellet.

Once there, I discover that even entire villages need a day of rest, as pretty much everything is closed! Thankfully, I uncover another bakery, almost as good as my regular haunt, and scare up walnut bread, olive bread and the last baguette. They also have a nice selection of quiches and savoury pastries on display, so a couple of those will round out lunch nicely.

Back home, leftovers are transformed into a potato salad and a beetroot salad, while our ever-expanding array of cheese gets a good workout.

At around 3 pm, Dad finally returns, greeted like the prodigal son. It takes me a while to register that he hasn't brought home any bread.

'Yeah, they don't have a bakery up there.' Right!

It is another dazzling afternoon, so Madeleine, Mum and the kids amble about in the heat, foraging.

MADELEINE: After the kids attempt to sample everything they encounter, from suspicious orange berries to clearly off-limits toadstools, we return with an impressive haul: Beurré Bosc pears, Cox, Russet and Golden Delicious apples, green figs with deep scarlet bellies, tiny blackberries at the end of their season, bundles of grapes, a couple of nearly ripe quinces, walnuts and, surprisingly, persimmons, growing from a huge tree, old as the hills, in the middle of the field. A real find, tucked away off a lane, is a crop of wild plums, tiny and honey-sweet.

I survey the pile of imperfectly shaped but utterly delicious bounty. For some reason the walnuts whisper most to me and I am off to the kitchen to prepare a parfait!

SAUTÉED CÈPES WITH APPLES AND WALNUT BREAD

Serves 4

Wipe the cèpes clean with a damp cloth and trim the bases of the stalks. Cut the cèpes into ½-cm-thick slices.

Warm a frying pan and fry the slices of the walnut bread in some of the clarified butter (or some olive oil) to a golden brown on both sides. Season with salt and pepper, then keep warm to one side.

Quarter the apples, peel and cut away the core with a paring knife. Cut each quarter into three, providing six slices per portion.

Heat the olive oil in the fry pan and, once hot, fry the cèpes for a few minutes on each side, to a rich golden brown. Add 1 tablespoon of the clarified butter, the shallots and garlic.

While the cèpes are sautéing, make the dressing by mixing the lemon juice and walnut oil with the vinegar and mustard. Season with salt and pepper. Add the herbs before serving.

Once the cèpes are ready, season with salt and pepper. Remove from the pan and keep warm.

Add the sliced apples and another tablespoon of clarified butter to the already hot pan. Stir for just a minute to warm the apples through before spooning them over the bread. The dish can now be finished with the dressing spooned over the mushrooms.

8 cèpes (12 if small)

4 slices walnut bread, about 2 cm thick

100 g clarified butter

salt and pepper

2 Russet or Golden Delicious apples

2 tablespoons olive oil

2 tablespoons finely chopped shallots

2 teaspoons crushed garlic

½ lemon, juiced

3 tablespoons walnut oil

2 tablespoons apple vinegar

1 teaspoon Dijon mustard

1 tablespoon chopped parsley

1 tablespoon chopped tarragon

½ bunch wild watercress

Wine

Château Simone from Palette is unusual in every respect. The vines are farmed on north-facing limestone rubble on the side of the Arc Valley, with a large range of grape varieties featured.

Palette is a tiny appellation in Provence of only 23 hectares, 17 of which belong to Château Simone and the rest are made up of pine forests. Simone is therefore the only vineyard in the appellation.

Their Grenache (45 per cent), blended with Mourvèdre and Cinsault, and 'secondary' grapes including Syrah and Castet, is an interesting wine.

The white is pretty good too, an unusual blend with Clairette predominant (80 per cent).

CHESTNUT PARFAIT
WITH WALNUTS AND HONEY

Serves 15

CHESTNUT PARFAIT
70 g caster sugar
10 egg yolks
250 g Mascarpone
500 g chestnut purée
500 ml pure cream
6 egg whites

WALNUT AND HONEY BISCUITS
225 g butter
125 g sugar
100 g glucose
15 g water
225 g honey
½ lemon, juiced
125 g flour
250 g chopped walnuts

GRANITA
100 g sugar
250 g water
1 vanilla bean, split and seeds scraped out
350 g Champagne
lime zest

CARAMEL SAUCE
300 g sugar
150 g cream
100 g butter

For the chestnut parfait, I advise to complete it 1 or 2 days in advance as this will ensure the cream freezes rock hard, which will make it easier to cut evenly.

For the chestnut parfait, mix half of the sugar with the egg yolks in a bowl.

Whisk on top of a bain-marie until the mixture reaches a frothy consistency and has doubled in size. Test by drawing the figure 8 into the top of the mixture: if the figure is still legible after 3–4 seconds, then the mixture has reached the required consistency.

Add the Mascarpone and chestnut purée, and whisk the mixture until both have dissolved. Leave the mix to one side to cool down.

Whip the cream to 'ribbon' stage, adding the remaining caster sugar as you go.

Once the mixture is cool, add the whipped cream—slowly, as we do not want the cream to split. Reserve 3 tablespoons in an airtight container for the final presentation.

Whip the egg whites using an electric mixer until they form soft peaks.

Gently add the beaten egg whites to the mixture, using a rubber spatula. Move from the bottom to the top, folding carefully.

Line a tray 1–2 cm deep, and 40 cm × 30 cm, with cling film or greaseproof paper and pour the mixture onto it. Freeze.

Leave for 1–2 days.

When frozen hard, cut into square pieces 5 cm × 5 cm.

Place the square blocks back in the freezer.

For the biscuits, place the butter, sugar, glucose, water and honey into a bowl, and then over a bain-marie to melt.

When these ingredients have melted, add the lemon juice, flour and chopped walnuts. Combine until the texture of the mix is smooth and creamy.

Place the mix in the fridge to rest for one hour.

Pre-heat the oven to 180°C.

Spread the mixture onto either a non-stick tray or a greaseproof-lined tray, spreading as thinly as possible.

Place the tray directly into the hot oven. Bake for approximately 6 minutes or until it has reached an appealing golden colour.

Remove from the oven and cool until it is comfortable to handle, but still warm and soft enough to cut with a knife. If the biscuit has set and is difficult to cut, place the tray back into the oven for 30 seconds.

Cut square pieces 5 cm × 5 cm—the same size as the parfait squares. You should have at least 45 squares.

Store the biscuits in an airtight container.

For the granita, start by placing the sugar and water into a suitable saucepan and bring to the boil. Add the seeds of the vanilla bean to the syrup.

When the syrup is boiling hot, add the Champagne and lime zest and cool down as quickly as possible. Pour into a deep dish and freeze.

Every 20 minutes, press and scrape the iced mix with a fork until fully frozen but aerated.

For the caramel sauce, caramelize the sugar until dark golden brown. Then add the cream and butter.

Take off the heat and mix till everything is incorporated. Cool down before use.

To assemble, top a biscuit with a square of the chestnut cream, followed by another layer of biscuit and chestnut cream, followed by a final layer of biscuit.

Place the creation at 3 o'clock on a plate. Leave in the freezer until required.

Place a scoop of the granita onto one corner. Serve immediately.

Day

11

Today we return to Gordes to show Mum and Dad the sights. With a little knowledge now under our belts, we get it right, making for a more enjoyable market experience all round.

A word to the wise: get there early! Last week we didn't arrive until after 11 am, coinciding perfectly with the market version of 'rush hour'. This time, we pull in before 9 am, park breezily close by and discover that the early bird doesn't have to pay for its car park! In fact, there is no one to be seen. I have to do a quick mental check that we have the correct day.

Cresting the hill, however, we see the market spread out, seemingly just for us.

MADELEINE: The *boucherie* is fully stocked and, before I can utter 'Un lapin, s'il vous plaît', a beautifully butchered bunny is in my bag. This is the same place where, last week, we couldn't even get in the door, the space being crammed with frenzied shoppers squabbling over the last cuts of meat.

Approaching the *boulangerie*, I can't believe it is empty. On our last visit, Shannon almost lost a limb for a croissant and a beignet. Today we load up on a few varieties of *pain*, custard *mille-feuille*, *pain au chocolat*, a mini hazelnut gâteau, a superb little strawberry tart and a fat, family-size *tarte tropézienne*.

The cobblestoned laneway earns its first curse from me about two feet out of the store. The pram bounces and the *tropézienne* shoots out on a journey all of its own. We salvage what we can, now more mush than *magnifique*.

We gather our ingredients from my favoured *paysan* stall: round, green courgettes for stuffing, Beefsteak tomatoes, *pêche plates*, figs, dates, red shallots, melon, raspberries, extra virgin olive oil hailing from Aureille, and shallot vinegar. This stuff is seriously good and makes any salad sing. Eggs, the always-in-demand butter and an artisanal orange cordial round out our purchases.

Now with some time on our hands before the hordes descend, and with a bag of fresh King Crab meat, I want to explore some of the wine stores. And though I don't purchase anything today, my understanding of Gordes' wine offerings is definitely more acute. The wine stores are uniformly impressive, but the prices can be a bit high.

Madeleine has been pointing the wine stores out since we arrived and it really hits home, in the midst of the Gordes marketplace, that there is a gulf that divides the *paysan* markets and stalls from their more commercial counter-parts: a passion for, and a deep knowledge of, their products that the stallholders are keen to share.

In our market experiences so far, the *paysan* community has been, to a man and woman, patient with us plodding along in broken French, encouraging us to comprehend *how* wonderful their product is, and *why* it is so wonderful. This stands in stark contrast to the larger markets, where most communication is just a prelude to the hard sell.

I suppose this is a commercial reality, but something about someone standing behind their tomato stall, both literally and figuratively, and showing the same measure of pride and joy in their products that they would in their own kids speaks to my heart. They have won my custom, and so I'll return every week to buy their tomatoes—rain, hail or shine.

It is by this simple equation that the *paysan* stallholder survives and thrives, thanks to the support of and devotion to the *paysan* tradition so apparent in this region. This tradition means tomatoes that are better for the planet, better for the conscience and absolutely better for the plate. It's really not that complicated after all, is it?

RED BELL PEPPER SOUP WITH CRAB MAYONNAISE

Serves 4

If the title of this recipe doesn't get the juices flowing, then please go and get help immediately. In Australia, we call red bell peppers capsicums, and for once we are right! The word derives from the Latin word *capsa*, meaning box or box-like fruit.

3 red bell peppers, cut in half and de-seeded

2 ripe tomatoes, roughly chopped

1 salad onion, roughly chopped

1 clove garlic

50 ml Heinz tomato ketchup

salt and pepper

50 ml white wine vinegar

1 cup olive oil

300 g picked King Crab

4 tablespoons mayonnaise

½ lemon, zested and juiced

8 baby or sheep sorrel leaves

other bay herbs such as saltbush or pig's face; optional)

Place the peppers, tomatoes, onion, garlic, ketchup, salt, pepper and vinegar in a blender and blend for 5 minutes until very smooth.

Strain the purée through a fine sieve. Whisk in the olive oil and adjust the seasoning. Refrigerate until needed.

On a tray, re-pick the crab to ensure there is no shell remaining, then add to a bowl along with the mayonnaise. Combine well and season with the lemon zest, salt, pepper and some of the lemon juice.

Form the crab into small balls; assume 5 balls per bowl.

Add the red pepper soup to each bowl, then float the crab balls on top of the soup. Add the sorrel and, if available, any other bay herbs on top. Serve.

BAKED RABBIT WITH LAVENDER AND MUSTARD, STUFFED COURGETTES

Serves 4

RABBIT

100 g Dijon mustard

2 teaspoons dried lavender

1 tablespoon fresh thyme leaves

2 tablespoons shallot vinegar (see below)

1 lemon, zested and juiced

1 cup olive oil

salt and pepper

1 × 2 kg farmed rabbit

COURGETTES

8 ball courgettes

2 tablespoons olive oil

salt and pepper

2 tablespoons fresh breadcrumbs

200 g black sausage (firm)

TO SERVE

cherry tomatoes, baked on their vine (optional)

For the rabbit, make a marinade by combining all the ingredients except the rabbit.

Add the rabbit and marinate for 2 hours.

For the courgettes, heat the oven to 180°C.

Cut off the top third of the courgettes. Reserve the tops as lids.

Scoop out the centres of the courgettes. Season the hollowed out courgettes with olive oil, salt and pepper.

In a food processor, add the breadcrumbs and black sausage, but only roughly combine the two together.

Stuff the courgettes with the mixture, top with the lids and place on a baking tray.

To finish, remove the rabbit from the marinade and place onto a separate baking tray or a spit to roast.

Bake the rabbit and courgettes for 30 minutes or until the rabbit is golden and the courgettes are cooked all the way through.

I like to serve with some baked cherry tomatoes still attached to the vine.

SHALLOT VINEGAR

Makes 1.2 litres

All chefs have little secrets and this is one I picked up many years ago while in France. The French take a huge amount of care with their vinegars and use the appropriate ones for different creations depending on the flavour profile. I believe shallot vinegar covers a large spectrum of the dishes requiring vinegar in Provence.

1 teaspoon pectin

1 litre white wine vinegar

8 brown shallots, peeled and finely minced

Dissolve the pectin in 1 cup of the vinegar by boiling in a pot.

Combine the pectin mixture with the shallots and the rest of the vinegar. Whisk together well and then store in small glass bottles. Use as required.

Wine

Perrin & Fils' 2001 Les Christins Vacqueyras is a mostly Grenache blend from quite a large vineyard owned by a cousin of Pierre Perrin.

The Famille Perrin are legends in the Luberon and Rhône valleys as they promote the quality of small growers and buy their grapes at very generous prices, thereby keeping properties in local hands for future generations.

Les Christins is lovely and spicy and slightly meaty. The taste is ripe and full and chocolaty, with a nice structure, open and sweetly fruited. Even though chocolate isn't something you would associate with rabbit or wine, this 10-year-old Vacqueyras worked well for us.

Wednesday, 14 September

Today is another of our regular forays along the D900
between Avignon and Apt, a length of road that we travel
pretty much regardless of our destination, be it Bonnieux,
Lourmarin, Roussillon, Oppède or Coustellet.

Every day we pass the local olive oil press, where the
villagers come to press and sell their olives. I hadn't yet
taken the time to stop and check it out. Today, as there is
nothing urgent on the agenda, I decide to drop by and pick
up some oil.

Back home with a bottle of cloudy, first-press oil, I
decide to whip up something sweet that really speaks of
Provence in late summer. Lemons from the market, local
lavender honey and olive oil combine to make a tasty
little cake you can serve dressed up or dressed down,
depending on your mood.

LEMON, HONEY AND OLIVE OIL CAKE

Serves 4

200 g caster sugar

3 eggs

salt

250 ml milk

250 ml extra virgin olive oil

3 lemons, juiced and finely zested

100 g honey

300 g plain flour, sifted

1 tablespoon baking powder

icing sugar

1 cup lavender essence (optional)

lavender flowers (optional)

vanilla-bean ice cream (optional)

Pre-heat the oven to 180°C.

Grease and flour a loaf cake tin.

Whisk the sugar, eggs and a pinch of salt in a mixer until thick and pale.

Combine milk, oil, lemon zest, lemon juice and honey in a large jug. Whisk together. Gradually add to egg mixture, whisking until just combined.

Fold through the flour and baking powder. Pour into the baking tin.

Bake for 25–30 minutes until golden and cooked through.

Cool in the tin for 5 minutes, then turn out and dust with icing sugar.

Serve warm or at room temperature.

For something extra special that really brings Provence into your kitchen, keep the still-hot cake in its tin and douse liberally with a cup of lavender essence. When cool, remove from the tin, dust with icing sugar and serve sprinkled with lavender flowers, beside a scoop of vanilla-bean ice cream.

Day

13

Today is Roussillon market and there are cèpes, figs and melons galore. I also locate some fresh Sea Bass fillets.

One tip worth remembering is that one should always get the female of the party to purchase anything that may be expensive when dealing with old market vendors.

Madeleine doesn't suspect a thing when I ask her to buy the cèpes. All I can see are three old blokes ogling her and telling her how beautiful she is! She then walks away glowing with a huge smile and I get these bloody amazing cèpes at half price. Everybody's a winner!

MADELEINE: The vendors at our stall of choice seem to have a weakness for Aussie women valiantly trying to wrestle with their language. The elderly men behind the stands indulge my attempts to stutter out my order, then take great delight in handing over what items they thought I'd requested—and a few extras for good measure, including a generous bundle of pristine cèpes, just gathered that morning from the outskirts of town, for next to nothing. *Magnifique!*

Now I have to work out what to do with all those cèpes!

CÈPES AND CHICKEN SALAD

Serves 4

1 cold roast chicken

4 tablespoons butter

8 medium cèpes
(or Paris mushrooms)

1 tablespoon capers

1 onion, finely diced

2 cloves garlic, crushed

1 cup Madeira
or sweet wine

2 tablespoons shallot
vinegar (see p. 97)

½ cup olive oil

1 tablespoon finely
chopped tarragon

½ lemon, juiced

4 cups of mixed
lettuce greens

Break the cold roast chicken down into 10 pieces, by removing the legs and halving them, then removing the breasts and halving them, and finally removing the wings and discarding the tips. Reserve the carcass for stock.

In a heavy-based fry pan, add 2 tablespoons of the butter. Heat the chicken with the skin side down. Season and reserve in a warm place.

Cut the bases of the cèpes off (you normally cut ⅛ off the base of a cèpe) and discard. Wash them quickly in warm water, rubbing off any mud or dirt. Dry the cèpes with a tea towel and slice them into ½-cm slices.

Place the fry pan over a high heat. Add the remaining butter to the pan and, as it starts to foam, add the cèpes. Fry until golden, then turn over and repeat. Season well.

Add the capers, diced onion and garlic, and cook for a further 2 minutes. Add the Madeira and reduce by two-thirds.

Add half the shallot vinegar and taste before adding more. Use the remaining vinegar as a seasoning.

Mix the olive oil, tarragon and lemon juice together with the salad leaves. Add these dressed leaves to the plate with 2 pieces of chicken per plate. Then add the mushrooms over the top.

Spoon over the warm pan juices and serve.

Wine

Château Val Joanis is a local Luberon producer in Pertuis.
Owner Jean-Louis Chancel makes great expressions of local
grape varieties under pretty tough AOC conditions. His Réserve
Les Aubépines, a blend of Grenache Blanc and Roussanne, is
a real winner with roast chicken and is a beyond-acceptable
match with this warm salad. The fresh and zingy 2009 has a
rich fruity palate with a hint of butter.

MEDITERRANEAN SEA BASS FILLETS
WITH ANTIBOISE SAUCE

Serves 4

4 Sea Bass, scaled and filleted

1 lemon, zested and juiced

1 orange, grated zest only

1 star anise, finely crushed

4 bay leaves

1 cup extra virgin olive oil

2 shallots, very finely diced

2 cloves garlic, crushed

2 large Beefsteak tomatoes, chopped

2 Green Zebra tomatoes, chopped

8 basil leaves

12 coriander leaves

12 picholine olives, pitted and quartered

1 teaspoon white peppercorns, crushed

salt

1 cup mussel juice (optional; see below)

In a large shallow dish, place the Sea Bass fillets with the lemon zest and orange zest, a pinch of star anise, bay leaves and half the olive oil. Refrigerate for 1 hour.

Place the remaining olive oil in a heavy-based fry pan. Add the shallots and garlic, and very gently sweat for 5 minutes without allowing them to colour.

Add the tomatoes, basil and coriander. Simmer for 3 minutes.

Add a few of the olives. Season with salt and freshly crushed white pepper, and the lemon juice.

Pre-heat a steamer or steaming pot large enough that the Sea Bass can be gently poached in the tomato sauce with a lid on. (This is my least preferable option to cook the fish, but it does work.)

Remove the Sea Bass fillets from the marinade. Add the marinade to the sauce in the steamer.

Poach the fillets for 3 minutes, then turn and cook for 3 minutes on the remaining side.

Blend the sauce in a blender until smooth. Adjust seasoning.

Spoon the tomato mixture onto four serving plates. Top each serving with a poached Sea Bass fillet, dress with some of the mussel juice, then dot with the remaining quartered olives.

SAUCE VIERGE

This Provençal sauce is really just a gently heated salad dressing, but a simpler and very useful replacement for the antiboise sauce (above). It is great with poultry too. I also love this with crayfish, served cold.

Place the oil, coriander seeds and garlic in a small pan. Warm gently for 10 minutes to infuse the flavours, then strain and discard the garlic and coriander seeds.

Add the tomatoes to the oil and soften.

Stir in the fruit juices, zest, basil and parsley. Season to taste.

1 cup extra virgin olive oil

10 coriander seeds

1 clove garlic, finely crushed

2 large Beefsteak tomatoes, de-seeded and cut into small dice

1 lemon, zested and juiced

1 grapefruit, zested and juiced

1 orange, zested and juiced

2 tablespoons julienned basil

1 tablespoon finely chopped flat-leaf parsley

MUSSEL JUICE

Put all the ingredients in a pre-heated pan and cook for 3–4 minutes, or until the mussels open.

Place in a colander over a bowl. Cover with cling film and let rest for 10 minutes.

Use mussel juice as appropriate. It will keep in the fridge for 1 or 2 days.

The mussels will be great as a light snack or in a salad.

1 kg mussels

¼ cup olive oil

½ bottle white wine

Wine

The 2007 Chateau Val Joanis Vigne du Chanoine Trouillet Grenache has soft rounded fruit with a touch of autumn earthiness. It is not the cheapest wine in the local *cave*, but at 15€ is a dream wine for the price.

PAN-FRIED BRIOCHE WITH THE LAST OF THE SEASON'S FIGS

Serves 4

1 loaf brioche
(approximately
20 cm × 10 cm)

500 ml milk

2 eggs

3 cups caster sugar

1 lemon, zested

½ cup brown sugar

4 tablespoons butter

8 figs, cut into quarters

¼ cup Grand Marnier

4 scoops of vanilla ice
cream

Trim all the crusts off the loaf of brioche, then cut the brioche lengthways into 4 even rectangles. Set aside.

In a saucepan over a low heat, bring the milk to simmer.

Combine the eggs, 2 cups of the caster sugar and lemon zest in a bowl, and whisk together.

Add one-third of the milk to the egg mixture and whisk together.

Add the egg mixture into the remaining milk on the stove, whisking rapidly.

When combined, stir slowly for 8 minutes or until the mixture slightly thickens. Remove from the heat and soak the brioche pieces in it for 30 minutes.

Pre-heat a large, heavy-based fry pan over a medium heat.

Place the brown sugar on a plate. Remove the brioche pieces and pat down on some paper towel. Proceed to coat the outside of the brioche with the sugar.

Add three tablespoons of the butter to the pan and then add the brioche pieces. Turn the heat down to low. Cook on each side until golden and crunchy. Remove from the pan and keep warm on separate plates.

Keep the pan on the stove and turn back up to a medium heat. Add the figs and the remaining tablespoon of butter. Cook quickly for 1 minute, as if you were sautéing a vegetable.

Add the Grand Marnier and reduce for one minute.

Spoon the figs and sauce over the toast and serve with a scoop of vanilla ice cream.

des journées entières dans les arbres

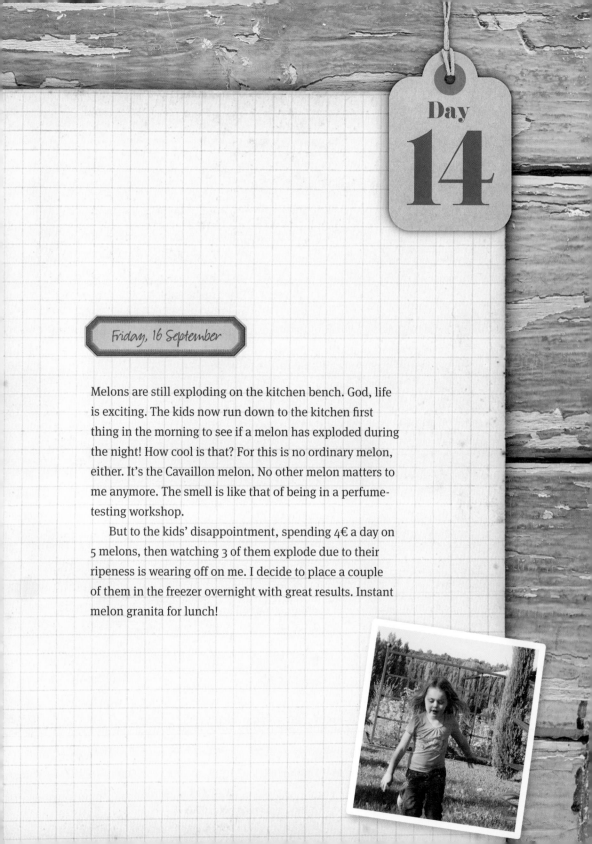

Friday, 16 September

Melons are still exploding on the kitchen bench. God, life
is exciting. The kids now run down to the kitchen first
thing in the morning to see if a melon has exploded during
the night! How cool is that? For this is no ordinary melon,
either. It's the Cavaillon melon. No other melon matters to
me anymore. The smell is like that of being in a perfume-
testing workshop.

But to the kids' disappointment, spending 4€ a day on
5 melons, then watching 3 of them explode due to their
ripeness is wearing off on me. I decide to place a couple
of them in the freezer overnight with great results. Instant
melon granita for lunch!

CAVAILLON MELON SOUP

Serves 4

2 Cavaillon melons,
halved and de-seeded

100 ml Chartreuse

2 tablespoons picked
lemon basil

1 lemon, zested and
juiced

salt and pepper

extra virgin olive oil for
drizzling

This is perfect for a hot day, especially for those of you who may not have tried a savoury melon soup before. If you are not in the South of France, rock melons will suffice. Just make sure they are ripe.

Cut the melons in half and scoop out most of the flesh with a melon baller. Place the balls in the freezer for 30 minutes.

With a dessertspoon, scoop out the melon that is left behind. Purée in a blender with the Chartreuse, fresh basil, lemon juice and zest, salt and pepper.

Pour the purée over the melon balls. Drizzle with a little olive oil and serve.

MELON GRANITA

2 melons, peeled and
de-seeded

½ cup Grand Marnier

100 g preserved or
candied ginger

¼ cup basil,
leaves picked

Take the melons and purée them. Add the Grand Marnier, and then place in a deep-sided tray and freeze overnight.

Scrape the frozen melon with a fork until it is fluffed up. This can be done in several stages throughout the day.

Add some finely chopped preserved or candied ginger and freshly ripped basil for a simple dessert.

It also makes a great addition to a Grand Marnier and Champagne cocktail.

Wine
....
Muscat de Beaumes-de-Venise!

Day
15

Another quick saunter down to a local *boulangerie* for a fortifying pastry to begin the day. This has become our routine and it is certainly not one I'm railing against. But, in spite of their irresistible deliciousness, these little butterballs are not the most energizing fuel upon which to start the day.

So, do the French really indulge in buttery *viennoiseries* for breakfast each day? *Boulangeries* are frequently overflowing with these goodies, so it is clear that they are being bought, but are they being purchased by locals or just by unsuspecting tourists like us, attempting to blend in with the scenery?

Croissants are your ultimate breakfast on the go: compact and portable. They are light on mess and fuss, besides the crumbs, and being devoid of sauces or drippy condiments they can be eaten literally 'on the run'. But perhaps judging a breakfast by these concerns is adhering too strictly to our eating culture back home. In France, breakfast tends to be a more leisurely affair, so the role of the pastry is more one of eating pleasure than convenience.

So, as to the question of whether the French dine on pastries for breakfast, the short answer is 'No, not regularly.'

Taking your morning repast in a café is de rigueur for the French, but the breakfast of choice is the *petit déjeuner*: coffee, juice, a length of baguette, butter and jam. At home, a Provençal is as likely to make do with a bowl of porridge as you and I are, with pastries reserved for more occasional indulgence.

MADELEINE: A buttery, fluffy little something seems to make its way onto the breakfast table everyday like clockwork, still fresh from the oven, warm and wafting its heavenly perfume about provocatively. I'm powerless to resist. Comforted by my mistaken belief our neighbours are doing likewise, I see no need to resist. Needless to say, my jeans are disgusted by my behaviour and, in a unified show of protest, are all refusing to zip up. One stubborn pair of hip-huggers won't even venture past my knees! Humbling, yes. Behaviour-modifying, no.

The French obviously succumb to temptation, because Jenny Craig has offices here, too.

Walnut trees are usually associated with the Dordogne region, but the Luberon is filled with them, and their fruit is an important part of the summer and autumn cuisine.

The trees are a source for both types of truffles found in the area. They really do add something to the atmosphere of being here in the late and early summer months.

One highlight for me on this trip so far comes when my children realize that walnuts come from a tree! Three-year-old Hendrix loves nuts and I get a lot of pleasure secretly watching him pick the whole nuts off the ground. Of course, if he knew I was watching, he would make me do it for him or get embarrassed and waddle off to play with Thomas the Tank Engine.

Later, Hendrix and his big sister Phoenix sit on the concrete steps with Dad and use rocks from the garden to crack them open—stopping to pick out the fresh nut, eat it, talk a little and then resume cracking. It is a defining moment and reminds me of how lucky I am.

PRESERVED WALNUTS

If you are fortunate enough to have your own fruiting walnut tree, or access to one, pick your green walnuts sometime in June—the earlier the better.

The size of the green walnut should be about the size of a very small egg. You should be able to cut it in half very easily and it should be a light green with a white sort of pith surrounding the half-developed walnut.

Peel the green round fruit with a potato peeler and place in water.

This recipe is great to serve with cheese or gamey terrines. The downside is that you need to soak the peeled walnuts in water for 4–5 days. Like purging an olive, change the water each day. And I recommend you do this in a wine cellar or the fridge.

Green walnuts, when cut open, leak a clear, colourless liquid which will very rapidly turn a dark brown and stain your fingers in such a way that it will remain there for several days, no matter how hard you try to remove it.

1 kg green walnuts, as per instructions above, peeled and cut in half

700 g caster sugar

700 ml water

2 cups lemon juice

1 cup orange juice

1 cinnamon quill

2 dried strips orange peel

2 dried strips lemon peel

salt

Blanch the walnuts in boiling salted water.

While this is happening, combine the sugar and fresh water in a copper saucepan. Bring to a boil over a high heat and then add in the drained, blanched walnuts. Bring to a boil again, and simmer the walnuts in the syrup for about 30 minutes.

Remove from the heat, place a lid on the saucepan and allow to steep for at least 2 hours. This is a variation of the confit technique.

Add the lemon juice, orange juice, cinnamon quill and dried peel to the syrup, and simmer for another 25 minutes.

Test a walnut to make sure they are cooked. The texture will be a bit like cooked carrots. If it's still too firm, cook it longer until it softens.

When the walnuts are ready, pour them and the syrup into sterilized jars and seal. Leave in the fridge for 30 days before serving. They should keep for at least 12 months in a cool, dark environment.

Sunday, 18 September

Truffles exist everywhere in France, but no region provides truffles scented with the aroma of oak trees quite like the Luberon. This is the winter variety, of course, for which I pay big money to serve in my restaurants.

I have always had a distain for any truffle other than the prized black winter truffle, *Tuber melanosporum*—that is, until I buy autumn truffles from the Coustellet market today. They are portioned out by the stallholder in little jam jars with the weight and price written on the lid like someone would label a jar of screws they had stored in their garage.

Pop the lid and the aroma is wow! The price is very cheap as well: 10€ will get you four truffles, enough to feed ten people. This is especially great value when you consider they were foraged for that morning on the hill behind our farmhouse.

The hill is full of dense patches of evergreen oak trees and the occasional walnut tree, limestone soils being conducive for the truffle, which spends its life underground, needing cold winters and warm summers to flourish.

The wild truffle is now scarce because the current economic climate is not conducive to the maintenance of forests or the proliferation of wild boars. Boars would feast on wild truffles and spread the spores through the forest, enabling the fungi to multiply over time.

It was not uncommon in the families of *caveurs* (the name given to the person who digs truffles in the woods) to set up roadside stalls and sell autumn truffle products such as terrines and truffled peaches in jars. In most parts of the world they are a delicacy, but not here in Provence, where the peasant is still king—or at least he eats like one.

A very grand and famous truffle festival takes place in Richerenches, known to locals as the truffle capital. It starts the winter truffle season in late November with the Ban des Truffles. There follows the first truffle market of the autumn, flanked by bored local men in ridiculous stockings, *Red Faces*–style ceremonial robes and hats.

Ménerbes also has a *maison de truffes* on top of the hill next to the old church. It sells all sorts of truffle products and has a 400-year-old wine cellar. The village has a small festival that changes dates each year depending on how successful the winter harvest is.

Carpentras is also very well known for truffle trading and it holds a Sunday truffle trading market each week during the season. By all reports it is a great spectacle and well worth a visit.

I head off instead to the Coustellet market, where I pick up the truffles, a fine duck for tomorrow's dinner and a slice or two of delicious pizza.

The word 'pizza' has always had an association with the Nice region of France, which until the mid-18th century was part of Italy. The tomato, olive and herb pizza has always been the speciality of this region and was originally called *socca* in the local dialect. Cheese is a modern addition.

Local people are very adamant that *socca* is a cross between the Italian pizza and the regional tartine. This is something that we as Australians can relate to: another country's influence that has evolved into a regional specialty.

Pizzas have been a surprise packet at most of the good bakeries. They are very thinly crusted, the toppings usually consisting of courgette ribbons and a tomato sauce or cooked onion, and half-melted anchovies. They surprisingly make a healthy breakfast snack.

PROVENÇAL PIZZAS

Makes 6 pizza bases

PIZZA STARTER
12 g dried yeast
80 ml warm water
220 g good flour

PIZZA DOUGH
1 teaspoon salt
600 g flour
250–300 ml water (room temperature)
1 quantity pizza starter (see above)
2 cups of flour for rolling and baking

Each of the portions of dough below should make a pizza base of about 22–26 cm in diameter. The size of each pizza is determined by how thick or thin the dough is rolled out. Don't worry if your pizza comes out a bit oblong, or even rectangular. The important thing is the thickness.

The dough should be as thin as possible—though the classic pissaladière is unusually thick—with the centre and edge being the same thickness.

I have tried varying the amount of water in the pizza dough. Less water will result in a less wet or tough dough, which is easier to make and roll out. It will also be slightly thicker when rolling the pizza. The use of more water will result in a very wet dough, which is harder to work with, but results in a crust much more like an authentic pizza. More flour will also be required when rolling out the dough.

Flour is very important to the success of a great pizza. A 'hard' unbleached flour is required. Look for specified bread flours in good providores.

For the starter, dissolve the yeast in the warm water and allow it to stand for approximately 8 minutes.

Add the flour and mix until a dough is formed.

Cover the starter with cling film and allow it to remain at room temperature for 1 hour.

For the dough, in a KitchenAid with the dough hook attached—or by hand—mix the salt with the flour. Add two-thirds of the specified water to the flour, then the starter.

Continue to mix the ingredients to the consistency of a soft dough. Knead the dough until it is smooth and elastic. This will take around 10 minutes.

Divide the dough into 6 equal portions. Shape each into a ball.

Dust a baking tray or wooden chopping board with flour. Place the 6 portions of dough on the flour-dusted surface. Cover with a towel and allow them to rise until double their original size. This depends on the ambient room temperature, but usually takes around 40 minutes. The proved portions can be kept in an airtight container stored below 4°C for several days, or frozen for several months.

Pre-heat the oven to 230°C.

If you are lucky enough to have a baking stone, pre-heat the stone for 20 minutes at this stage or even earlier. If there is no baking stone available for your oven, choose a heavy-based oven tray and pre-heat the tray the same way as a stone. If two ovens are available, use both to speed up the process of making all 6 pizzas.

Place each portion onto a floured work surface. Roll the edge of each portion of dough toward the centre, kneading it gently, while maintaining a round shape using either a bottle of wine or rolling pin. Don't be too concerned if the base is not perfectly round. What's important is that there are no holes and it has an even thickness (thin).

Finish with the two suggested toppings below.

SUMMER TRUFFLE AND BROUSSE DU ROVE PIZZA

Serves 4

3 rolled pizza bases

2 sprigs thyme

1 teaspoon rosemary

½ cup olive oil

100 g Brousse du Rove, sliced very thinly

20 g summer truffles, sliced as thin as possible

salt and pepper

Summer truffles are rarely worth cooking with, but they work well for this recipe. They don't have a strong flavour and need to be sliced very thinly. Olive oil helps intensify their flavour.

(If you don't want to eat them on pizza, another good tip is to use dried cèpes and make them into a purée with button mushrooms, shallots and garlic. Place it all into a pan with some olive oil and deglaze with some sweet wine, then purée with a finely chopped truffle.)

Place each pizza base onto a well-floured tray that will be easy to slide off onto the hot stone or tray in the oven.

Sprinkle the herbs liberally over the bases.

Liberally sprinkle olive oil over the bases. Be generous.

Place slices of the cheese over the bases, most probably 5 per base.

Include the crust of the cheese as it gives the pizza character.

Season well and slide onto the pre-heated stone or tray. Bake for around 5 minutes.

When crisp, remove from the oven and add the truffles.

Slice and serve.

PISSALADIÈRE

Serves 4

It is best to make this topping in advance—ideally at least an hour before baking or up to 1 day ahead of time.

4 tablespoons olive oil

3 brown onions, thinly sliced

3 cloves garlic, finely chopped

3 bay leaves

1 teaspoon freshly picked thyme

1 tablespoon drained capers

1 large rolled pizza base (see above)

16 anchovy fillets

20 niçoise olives

salt and pepper

Heat 3 tablespoons of the olive oil in a large, heavy skillet over medium-low heat. Add the onions, garlic, bay leaves and thyme. Stir to blend.

Cover and cook until the onions are very tender, stirring occasionally, for about 45 minutes.

Uncover and sauté about 10 minutes longer, or until most of the liquid evaporates and the onions are golden.

Stir in the capers. Season the mixture with salt and pepper and leave to the side.

Place the pizza base onto a well-floured tray that will be easy to slide off onto the hot stone or tray in the oven.

Liberally sprinkle the remaining olive oil over the base.

Place generous quantities of the onion mix over the base, most probably 5 tablespoons.

Place the anchovies and olives in a decorative pattern, and season well.

Slide onto the pre-heated stone or tray and bake for around 5 minutes. When crisp, remove from the oven.

Slice and serve.

MADELEINE: The day dawns cold with a bitter wind that whips about the house, rattling windows, slamming doors, echoing down corridors and putting the willies up everyone generally. It is a perfect day to curl up with a book ... or a lobe of foie gras!

There are no markets nearby and no one feels like stepping out the front door. But with our olive oil supply exhausted with yesterday's pizza making, and the bread barrel empty, someone will have to journey out eventually.

Not the best of drivers even on terra firma back home, I have willingly banned myself from taking the wheel here. The challenges presented by driving on the opposite side of the road just seem too big to overcome and, with my penchant for driving at either a snail's pace or putting the pedal to the metal, could evoke some serious road rage from the impatient French drivers we have encountered already.

Accordingly, with a deep air of drama, I offer to walk to Ménerbes for bread. Thank goodness Shannon had already swallowed his mouthful of coffee prior to this announcement as there was a fair chance he would have been wearing it. 'Madeleine? ... walk? ... to Ménerbes? Have I missed something? Have Arsenal been dropped from the Premier League and this is her way of soothing the blow?'

But, no, I am serious. Off I trundle, backpack in position, with the air of a battle-scarred hero returning to the front. Shannon, I suspect, thinks I am only going so that I can control the bread order, pushing for the dense, rough-hewn grain *boules* and *pain aux céréales*, with a buttery olive *fougasse* on the side. He's more of a baguette man, appreciative of the clean lines and honest flavour, along with the almost architectural perfection of the humble croissant.

There is a certain jittery slant to my walk when I return up the driveway some 90 minutes later, empty-handed with nary a beignet in sight. With a voice teetering on hysteria, I announce that the little market we frequent in Ménerbes has run out of bread and, being a Monday, the *boulangerie* is closed! This last fact is delivered with that particular rolling of the eyes common to horses on the verge of a stampede.

Until that moment, I don't think any of us had realized how married we had all become to Provence's incredible bread. Back in Australia, with the 24/7 availability of admittedly poor-quality bread, and bread-chain outlets springing up on every corner, the notion of buying bread each day is quite alien. If we don't have any, we don't have any.

But here, fresh *pain* is just that: fresh, designed to be consumed the same day of purchase or transformed into breadcrumbs the next. It is a significant component of every meal, and its texture and aroma alone are enough to set the mouth watering.

So, we head off to Coustellet. Sure enough, our favourite baker has shut up shop for the day. This place boasts a bread oven so good it has its own tribute window on the shop's exterior, with photos and declarations dedicated to its brilliance. This is a town that loves its bread.

We circle aimlessly, slowly gravitating toward the supermarket with heavy hearts, though it must be said even the supermarkets here do a decent line of fresh bread. For the most part it is preservative-free and baked on the premises.

Providence then intervenes and I spot a little place on a quiet corner with stacks of *palmiers* in the window. Inside, their range is extremely limited (it is noon by this time) but truly exquisite: baguettes with the crisp golden crust and subtle bubbling that trumpet the excellence of the baker's craft and the quality of the ingredients; long *epi* loaves, with a rustic assembly that makes each loaf resemble an enormous wheat stem; delicate croissant and pain au chocolat; and a texturally unusual *mais* or corn bread with a marbling achieved by loosely folding together wheat and corn flours before baking.

The loaves are still hot, almost too warm to handle, and release little puffs of steam when broken open. The smell is like a grandmother's: embracing, full of love, generous and nurturing.

Back home, lunch is just a matter of putting a bit of whatever is in the fridge on a wedge of chewy, crunchy deliciousness. A little butter will suffice—or, as Hendrix demonstrates, a hunk ripped from the loaf and stuffed straight in the mouth is all the sustenance one needs.

With dinner still to prepare (I have the duck I bought yesterday to contemplate), I am inspired to drag out the flour and yeast again, and put on my baker's apron for the afternoon.

Brioche is on the cards, and I'm curious to see if my efforts, with an average domestic kitchen oven, can stand up against the baking mastery we have encountered so far.

This is a country that stands by its bread, celebrates its pâtisseries and even has photomontages dedicated to its bread ovens!

OLIVE OIL BRIOCHE

Recipe by Michel Troisgros

Combine the flour, caster sugar, yeast and salt in a large mixing bowl. Using a mixer with the dough hook attached, mix to combine the ingredients.

Add the orange blossom water and milk, and mix on a low speed to form a dough.

Double the speed and continue mixing until the dough comes away from the sides of the bowl.

Reduce the speed and slowly add the olive oil a little at a time, beating well between each addition to ensure the mixture does not split.

Transfer the dough to a lightly oiled container twice the size of the mixture. Cover with plastic wrap and rest at room temperature for 1 hour, then in the fridge for 1 hour. The dough will double in size.

Place the dough on a floured work surface and knead for 1 minute.

Divide the dough into 50 g portions and shape by hand into balls.

Place the balls onto a tray lined with baking paper and cover with cling wrap.

Pre-heat the oven to 170°C.

Place the tray in a warm spot in the kitchen until the balls have doubled in size—about 90 minutes.

Brush the rolls gently with egg wash and bake in the oven for 20 minutes until golden brown.

Remove from the oven and allow to cool on a wire rack.

250 g plain flour

40 g caster sugar

14 g dry yeast

1 pinch salt

80 g orange blossom water

40 g organic milk

125 g extra virgin olive oil

1 egg yolk mixed with water, for egg wash

SLOW-COOKED DUCK WITH HONEY AND THYME

Serves 4

1 large farm-raised duck

2 banana shallots, diced

4 sprigs Provençal thyme

8 small to medium carrots, sliced

4 turnips, peeled and quartered

salt and pepper

¼ cup shallot vinegar (see p. 97)

3 tablespoons honey

2 quinces, peeled and cut into 6 pieces each

1 litre chicken stock

Pre-heat the oven to 160°C.

Break up the duck into pieces, firstly removing the legs and cutting each in half. Then remove the 2 breasts. Chop up the carcass with a meat cleaver into 4–5 pieces.

Heat a Le Creuset casserole dish over a medium heat. Using no oil or seasoning, roast off the duck pieces skin-side down only, starting with the breasts. After each batch of rendering, drain the fat off into a container and keep for other dishes.

Once this task is complete, add the duck carcass pieces into the pan and continue to brown off. Add the shallots, thyme, carrots and turnips. Season well with salt and pepper.

Add the shallot vinegar and cook rapidly for 30 seconds. Then add the honey and bring to the boil.

Add the quinces and stock. Bring to the boil, cover with a lid and place into the oven for 2 hours.

Remove and serve with crusty bread and braised Swiss chard (see below).

Wine

The 2000 Château Vignelaure is one of the finds of the whole stay. I paid 25€ from the *cave* in Lourmarin, which I think is a real bargain.

Made from Cabernet, Grenache and Syrah, it is harvested from aged vines under low yields. Crafted to drink young, but with 10 years' age, it becomes a classy Bordeaux-style wine reminiscent of what the original owner, Georges Brunet, also achieved at Château La Lagune in the Médoc. During his time there, Georges put the estate firmly on the vinous map.

Château Vignelaure is situated in Rians, which is close to the beautiful town of Aix-en-Provence. On the road to Rians from Aix, you pass the majestic mountain of Mont Sainte-Victoire, which was famously painted by Cézanne.

BRAISED SWISS CHARD WITH PASTIS (BETTES À LA MARSEILLAISE)

Serves 4

1 kg Swiss chard

olive oil

1 medium shallot, finely chopped

2 cloves garlic, finely chopped

1 tablespoon pastis

400 ml chicken stock, reduced to 80 ml

220 ml cream

50 g Emmenthal cheese, grated

salt and pepper

Pre-heat the oven to 190°C.

Prepare chard ribs by removing the leaves. Wash and cut into pieces about 3 cm long.

Cook the ribs in boiling salted water for 10 minutes.

Heat a heavy Le Creuset or heavy-based casserole dish with a little olive oil over a medium heat. Add the chard leaves, shallot and garlic, then the pastis. Reduce, then add the chicken stock and cream, salt and pepper. Boil, then remove from the heat.

Micro-plane the Emmenthal cheese over the braised chard.

Place in the oven for 5–10 minutes.

Serve in the dish.

FIGS WRAPPED IN OLIVE OIL BRIOCHE

Serves 6

½ quantity raw olive oil brioche dough, proved (see p. 133)

6 purple figs

1 egg yolk mixed with water, for egg wash

4 tablespoons lavender honey

2 tablespoons almond meal

1 punnet of raspberries

6 scoops of pistachio or vanilla ice cream

Pre-heat the oven to 160°C.

Divide the brioche dough into 6 equal pieces and roll them out to 4 mm thick.

Place the figs in the centre of each rolled-out disc of brioche.

Fold the brioche dough upwards, sealing against the stem of the fig. Then let the wrapped figs prove for 20 minutes.

Brush generously with the beaten egg wash and place the six wrapped figs into a buttered or baking paper–lined flan dish. Put into the oven and bake for 15 minutes.

Whilst they continue to bake, pour over the honey.

After 15 minutes, sprinkle with the almond meal. Bake for a further 5 minutes.

Serve while still hot with raspberries and a scoop of ice cream.

Originating from the *Capparis spinosa* and native to the coast of the Mediterranean Sea, capers were originally not salted but stored in olive oil, where, over a few months, they would develop in flavour and go slightly soft. Locals would then serve them in a bowl with bread as a simple meal. This, I suspect, is where the local tapenade originated.

Capers are a food staple of the Luberon area. The most common way of storing them here is in salted water. Some shopkeepers have local suppliers who deliver them in sea salt. They are then charged per 50 grams.

I prefer the Lilliput variety, which is very small and doesn't require chopping. I just add them straight to whatever recipe I'm cooking. But they are not available in this region. I have only ever come across a small-to-medium size.

I asked the caretaker of the farm where we are staying and he tells me the local ones come from the same caper plant, but they are all very old and this may have something to do with their size. Despite their size, they are delicious and not the least bit overpowering. These capers are firm but not hard, juicy but not soggy, and have a lovely salty after-taste.

THE ORIGINAL TAPENADE

200 g black or picholine pitted olives (I use a mix of both), roughly chopped

180 g can quality tuna (albacore) in extra virgin olive oil

3 shallots, peeled and roughly chopped

60 g capers, drained and rinsed

2 cloves garlic, crushed

1 lemon, halved

salt and pepper

1 cup olive oil

Add all the ingredients (except lemon juice, salt, pepper and olive oil) to the bowl of a food processor.

Squeeze over a generous flow of lemon juice (to taste), and equally generous grinds of salt and pepper.

Begin to process, pouring in the olive oil until the mix is well blended and glossy.

Wednesday, 21 September

Off to Marseille today to pick up my brother Liam. He is a handy photographer as well as a commercial airline pilot and is assisting me on this book. He is on a late-afternoon flight from Paris, so who knows when he will get here but, in anticipation, I am dragging the clan there for some much needed sea air and plenty of Omega 3.

I also want to try to have a decent bouillabaisse at Miramar, the favourite Marseille restaurant of *Los Angeles Times* food writer Clifford Wright. He says the use of Scorpion Fish—and the crucial step of having the water boiling before any fish is added—is best executed here. Let's see!

But first I need to set the record straight: I always thought bouillabaisse was invented on a beach somewhere near Marseille, overlooking the Mediterranean under a beautiful sunset, by some severely undernourished but creative fisherman.

Trying to come terms with my flourishing imagination has led me to believe that I'm gullible. Wright has consistently mentioned bouillabaisse over the past decade and

I have become fascinated with how he has dug out the past to discover the evolution of the fish stew, and how the bouillabaisse stands out from other countries' 'interpretations' or evolutions. The use of saffron, spices and quality fish has led the soup to become a meal, and to separate itself from other variants found in Mediterranean countries.

When we get to Marseille, I find Miramar is fully booked out and all I can do is merely quote from Clifford Wright on the history of the famous stew, broth or soup:

> In Claude François Achard's *Dictionnaire de la Provence et du Comté-Venaissin* the word bouilhe-baisso is defined as 'a fisherman's term, a sort of ragout consisting of boiling some fish in seawater.' This may be so, but this is a far cry from the bouillabaisse we know of today with its saffron, fennel, orange zest, and Pernod and expensive fish such as Rascasse (Scorpion Fish).

Instead of Miramar, we go to the café on the corner next to the chemist in Le Port Rouge. It is packed with locals and has a great atmosphere. I don't have the bouillabaisse after all that, but a delicious variation.

This fun lunch made me glad we have come to Marseille ... that and getting to see my brother, of course!

BOURRIDE

Serves 4

Bourride is the quintessential Provençal fish soup. It is a cheaper sister of the bouillabaisse, and way less complicated, but nowhere near as complex in taste.

There are various local variations. In the Luberon, they seem to use any white fish available at the market. Monkfish is going for 11€ a kilo at the Bonnieux market. That will do nicely.

The Apt market on Saturdays has a stall actually selling the finished soup. I am assuming that the locals consume the soup on site, but I cannot be sure as the containers in which the soup is sold are very large. But my God are they cheap! A litre container of ready prepared *bourride* is about 3.50€. It also makes me laugh when I watch the stallholder prepare a new batch in a 100-litre aluminium drum pot that looks like it was built for a World War II submarine kitchen. Who needs fancy pots!

In Marseille, they use a mixture of Monkfish and Merlan, which is the Mediterranean version of Whiting. Some people serve the broth on its own, followed by the fish and vegetables with boiled potatoes and aioli. You can put slices of bread in bowls and pour the soup over the fresh bread.

If a dinner party is in order, I would split this soup up into 2 courses. Serve the broth on the side and possibly add carrots to the recipe.

---

3 large Beefsteak tomatoes, roughly chopped

1 medium-sized fennel, roughly chopped

2 onions, roughly chopped

5 cloves garlic, peeled and roughly chopped

2 sprigs thyme

1 pinch saffron

1 orange, zest removed with a knife and cut into thin strips

1 cup olive oil

½ bottle white wine

500 ml fish stock or water

800 g filleted Monkfish or other firm, white fish

16 small potatoes, boiled and peeled after cooking

4 tablespoons *rouille* (see p. 147)

1 cup toasted ripped bread (see p. 148)

salt and black pepper

In a large pan, bring to the boil the tomatoes, fennel and onions, garlic, thyme, saffron, orange zest, about ½ cup of the olive oil, white wine and stock or water. Simmer for 20 minutes.

Meanwhile, cut each piece of Monkfish into 3 or 4 pieces, approximately 30 g each. Try to keep the pieces more or less the same size to ensure even cooking.

Add the fillets to the poaching liquid, lower the heat and simmer very gently for about 5 minutes. Be careful not to overcook the Monkfish. It loses all of its appeal when dry. Season to taste.

Place 4 potatoes into each bowl. Ladle the soup evenly over the potatoes.

Drizzle the remaining olive oil over each bowl. Add some rouille and croutons before serving.

PROVENÇAL FISH BROTH WITH ROUILLE *Serves 4*

1/3 cup olive oil

2 Scorpion Fish, de-scaled and filleted (keep the bones)

2 small Red Mullet, de-scaled and filleted (retain the bones)

500 g baby mussels, washed

3/4 bottle white wine

2 large banana shallots, peeled and finely chopped

5 cloves garlic, peeled and crushed

1 small fennel bulb, finely chopped

2 large Beefsteak tomatoes, finely chopped (use juices and seeds)

2 teaspoons pimentée sauce (see p. 83)

1 lemon, juiced and finely zested

1/4 bunch tarragon, finely chopped, including stems

4 large scallops, de-shelled, washed and diced

4 tablespoons rouille (see below)

1 cup toasted ripped bread (see p. 148)

This recipe is not a bouillabaisse. I am out to recreate what I think a local fisherman would have made on the beach in a simple cast-iron pot over a small campfire. I'm sure no wine would have made it into the cooking, but just ignore that part. Scorpion Fish can be replaced with Gurnard in Australia.

In a large pot over a medium heat, add 1 tablespoon of the olive oil and fry the fish bones. Cook them until they are golden in colour—about 2 minutes each side.

Turn up the heat to high and add the mussels. Stir several times whilst still retaining the high heat.

Add the white wine and immediately cover the pot with the lid. Boil for 2 minutes.

Strain the soup through a colander and retain. Discard the fish bones and retain the mussels in a bowl covered with cling film.

When cold, pick the mussels, removing the beards by pulling them out of the mussels and discard the shells.

Return the mussel stock to the saucepan and place back on the stove on a medium heat. Add the shallots, garlic, fennel and tomatoes. Simmer for 10 minutes.

Add the pimentée sauce, lemon juice and zest, and tarragon. Simmer for a further 5 minutes, taste and adjust seasoning.

Warm some soup bowls.

While the broth is simmering over a medium heat, add some olive oil to a fry pan over a medium heat and season the fish fillets well. Place them in the hot pan, skin side down, and cook until golden on the skin.

Turn over and cook for a further 30 seconds.

Place 2 fillets in each warm bowl.

Just before serving the broth, divide the diced scallops and picked mussels equally between each bowl. Ladle over the broth, then spoon over some rouille and toasted ripped bread.

Serve.

ROUILLE

Makes enough for 2 recipes

Combine the saffron and lemon juice together for 5 minutes to leach the colour from the saffron.

Place all the ingredients except the oil into a food processor or bowl and combine well. Either whilst whisking, or as the food processor is operating slowly, add the oil in the same fashion as you would to make a mayonnaise.

Once thick and yellow in colour, it is ready.

I prefer to leave it out at room temperature for 30 minutes before serving to allow the saffron to permeate the oil and eggs.

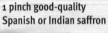

1 pinch good-quality Spanish or Indian saffron

½ lemon, juiced

2 egg yolks

2 eggs, boiled for 12 minutes and finely mashed

1 medium potato, cooked, peeled and mashed (do not refrigerate)

2 tablespoons Dijon mustard

1 tablespoon Champagne vinegar

salt and pepper

1 teaspoon pimentée sauce (optional)

1½ cups olive oil

TOASTED RIPPED BREAD

day-old round loaf of bread
olive oil
1 clove garlic, peeled
salt and pepper

Remove the crusts from the bread with a bread knife. Using your fingers, rip the bread into bite-size pieces

Over a medium heat, pan-fry the bread with a small amount of olive oil. Fry until partly crispy on most sides.

Remove and rub each nugget of bread with the garlic clove once or twice. Season and serve.

AIOLI (GARLIC SAUCE)

2 starchy, medium-sized potatoes
2 heads red garlic
salt and pepper
2 cups olive oil
½ lemon, juiced

Garlic in France is a seasoning. Nearly all recipes that involve onion also involve garlic. I actually think garlic exists to make onions taste good. Scandinavians will defiantly disagree, but I don't care. It's my opinion and I have so many garlic cloves lying around that I feel I will have dishonoured my faith in Provençal cookery if I don't serve another course before the real course!

Aioli is perfect for this. Present it with crisps—or, as we Aussies like to put it, 'chips'—or a grilled piece of fish.

The locals like to use fresh vegetables, so I'll follow with fresh radishes and tomatoes cut into eighths lengthways. They are from Collin's garden, with his permission of course!

Please use a mortar and pestle to crush the garlic. The resulting texture makes me feel that our world has not yet been taken over by automated factories!

Pre-heat the oven to 150°C.

Place the potatoes and garlic on a tray with salt and pepper, and a drizzle of the olive oil. Seal the tray in some aluminium foil. Place into the oven and bake for 50 minutes.

Peel the skin off the garlic and potatoes. Discard the skins.

Either in a food processor or with a mortar and pestle, blend the garlic and potatoes with the olive oil and lemon juice, and season.

Serve at room temperature as a dip.

Alternatively, it makes a great base for a simple pizza topping.

BABY FENNEL COOKED IN FISH STOCK AND SAFFRON

Serves 4

Yet another fish stock variation, this one is enriched with baby fennel.

I love to serve it with scallops wrapped in bacon strips. Add the scallops to the dish 4 minutes before serving. If scallops are not an option, a simple pan-fried fillet of fresh local fish will do just nicely.

Place the fennel, garlic, saffron, smoked bacon and fish stock in a large shallow pan. Bring to the boil, boil rapidly and reduce by two-thirds or until the stock starts to become a glaze.

Add the tarragon and olive oil, and season well. Continue to boil until the fennel has a beautiful glossy appearance and the taste is intense.

12 baby fennel

2 cloves garlic, crushed

2 pinches saffron

100 g finely chopped smoked bacon (*ventrèche*)

500 ml fish stock

¼ cup tarragon, finely chopped

¼ cup olive oil

salt and pepper

Phoenix, who has taken to proudly announcing she wants
to be a vet *and* a chef (slight conflict of interest there, but I
hate to dent her enthusiasm), has taken to whiling away the
quiet afternoons collecting a menagerie of creepy crawlies
and installing them in purpose-built nests as her 'friends'.
She gathers treats of brightly coloured flowers, which she
arranges lovingly about their new homes, croons lullabies
to them, narrates amazing adventures starring them and
bestows them with loving names such as 'Splotty' the worm,
'Choochoo' the beetle and 'Ramadam' the stick insect.

Favoured captives in her play are the tiny white snails
we find scattered high on the stems of plants, like a carpet
of little white flowers. With their pretty alabaster shells, we
just dismissed them as another quaint garden creature. It
was only today, while flicking idly through an old provincial
cookbook in an antiques stall, that I discovered they are
edible and, following a very Provençal preparation, make a
sweet little snack unique to Marseille.

The snails, *limaçon* (or *escalo fenoum*, their Provençal name, given for their habit of congregating at the top of fennel plants), are sold by the shopkeepers of Marseille in little paper cones. They suggest cooking them in water with lots of herbs and spices, then eating them—shell and all!

I prefer steeping them slowly in a court bouillon, before lightly sautéing in garlic, eschalot, butter and whatever fresh herbs I have on hand. Finish with a generous grind of salt and pepper, and a squeeze of lemon juice, and serve with the pan juices and fresh bread. A lively little starter with a satisfying crunch!

SNAILS WITH GARLIC AND WHITE WINE, AND A TARRAGON EMULSION

Serves 6

100 g butter

6 fresh cloves garlic, crushed

36 cooked and picked snails (*petits gris*)

salt

1 cup white wine

tarragon emulsion (see below)

Heat a pan over a high heat and melt the butter. Add the garlic and turn the heat to a low, gentle flame.

Add the snails and sauté for 3–4 minutes. Season with salt and turn up the heat to high.

After 30 seconds, making sure not to burn the butter or garlic, add the white wine.

Boil the snails and wine for 3–4 minutes until they have emulsified to form a glaze around each snail.

Remove the snails and their juices from the pan into a bowl. Place a toothpick or skewer into each snail.

Evenly pipe or teaspoon some of the tarragon emulsion into mounds on a flat platter. Place a snail with the skewer into each mound of tarragon emulsion.

Serve.

TARRAGON EMULSION

Serves 6

1 bunch tarragon (picked leaves only)

1 shallot, finely diced

1 garlic clove, crushed

500 ml chicken stock, reduced to 100 ml

75 ml apple vinegar

300 ml olive oil

¼ cup torn white bread

pinch of salt

This dip will need to be served at room temperature or directly from the fridge as it has a tendency to split when exposed to high heat. It also works well as a beautiful accompaniment to home-made chips.

Place the tarragon, shallot, garlic, chicken stock and apple vinegar in a blender. Blend until smooth.

With the blender still running, slowly add the olive oil to allow the oil to emulsify without splitting. When complete, add the bread to thicken. Blend for a further 30 seconds, using the pulse function to allow the bread to blend without forming lumps.

Season with a pinch of salt.

We drive once more along the stunningly beautiful but very
narrow and congested road to Lourmarin. We are having
lunch at Reine Sammut's famous hotel-restaurant at the
Auberge la Fenière. It is located 2 kilometres outside of the
village and is without doubt the best dining experience for
kilometres around.

The moment you enter the grounds of the hotel,
you immediately gain a sense of *terroir*, Provençal time
momentarily standing still as you pick up the aromas of
wild herbs wafting between the fruit trees.

I have not stayed here, but the 12 rooms look amazing.
Most have views of the Durance Valley. I'm a terrible
candidate for being a romantic, but I do find this place
makes even the staunchest of blokes become slightly
romantic. It's the combination of the colours, the blue skies
and the sense of knowing your better half is content.

The hotel has a cooking school, a providore, wine
tastings and a stunning little bistro, La Cour de Ferme,
housed in the original farmhouse, that is open only for

dinner, plus an amazing array of little tables scattered around the expansive gardens.

Reine Sammut was destined to become a lawyer before she met her husband, Guy, who with his mother trained her in the art of being a chef and host. She reminds me of a French Stephanie Alexander: passionate, humble and driven. Her food tastes of the love and passion for ingredients.

There is a strong push for establishing the cuisine as '*terroir* of the Luberon', but it sways here into other Provençal dialects with such classics as *bourride* and even a touch of North African spice.

The à la carte menu is the way to go for lunch, especially on a stunning summer's day sitting on the terrace. Dishes such as Turbot Cooked with Lentils and Lemongrass are simply that: great ingredients, with a touch of class to the presentation.

Madeleine orders a local Butternut Squash Velouté with Seared Duck Foie Gras, Porcini, Smoked Bacon Dice and Wild Herbs. The soup comes to the table in a large clay pot and is served, then the pot is left at the table—a big mistake with Madeleine around!

I have a Crab Ravioli with a Creamy Velouté and Red Mullet Roe Emulsion. It is one of the greatest entrées I have eaten in recent times.

As you would expect, desserts and cheese are well worked. I have frozen *calissons* served with apricot and bitter almond coulis, which is a really nice modern take on a classic local marzipan sweet that is normally eaten with tea or coffee. Madeline goes for the iced soufflé with citrus, exotic fruits and crunchy caramel. She says nothing, just eats, which means it must be utterly delicious!

I highly recommend this restaurant for its simplicity and element of not caring if you don't like it. I'm sure their motto is: 'This is our family home. It is what it is. Please enjoy and always smile.'

On the way home from Reine Sammut's, I stop at a second-hand bookseller in the village, where I find some wonderful old cookbooks. There are plenty of recipes I want to try immediately, but after such a lunch all we can manage for dinner are simple omelettes and home-made *calissons*.

OMELETTES

Omelettes are made in a different style all over the world, but many regard Provence as the home of the omelette.

Several 13th-century records suggest eggs were baked here in flat earthenware dishes. These simple egg dishes were called *lamelle*, meaning thin strips, and that eventually evolved by the 15th century into the word *amelette*.

Presentation still retains the same tradition today, omelettes being open-faced to showcase the wonderful different fillings. They are similar in presentation to a thin pizza in many ways. In other parts of France, they fold the omelette.

The locals also add a dash of water to the beaten eggs. This makes the omelette a little softer in terms of texture.

The other main difference is the use of olive oil instead of butter to cook the omelette in. Provençals also don't mind a little colour on the bottom of the omelette, but prefer none on the top.

The classic 'celebratory' omelette is called the *Le Crespeou*. It is a complicated layering of several vegetable-filled omelettes stacked on top of each other to form a sort of *mille-feuille*. It is served cold on buffets with salads at celebratory times during the warmer months, like Bastille Day. There can be as many as 20 layers.

An old recipe I discovered contains artichokes, aubergines, tomatoes, courgette flowers, white onions, green and red peppers, cèpes, herbs, tapenade and anchovies. It calls for 50 eggs to be used. Now that's an omelette!

I always like to season my omelettes in the cooking process as little as possible. I find salt is essential to the taste of great egg, but not to the texture. It seems to make the egg less delicate.

Here are four recipes I serve in the middle of the table in big, old cast-iron pans.

WILD MUSHROOM AND
SUMMER TRUFFLE OMELETTE *Serves 2 as a main meal*

Pre-heat the oven to 100°C.

Over a high heat, add some of the oil to a heavy cast-iron pan. Add the onion, garlic and girolles, and sauté for one minute.

Season well and add the parsley, butter and a squeeze of lemon juice.

Sauté a further 30 seconds or until steam appears from the pan. This will indicate water is starting to dissipate from the mushrooms.

It's important not to overcook the mushrooms as they will become flavourless.

Remove and drain on paper towel. Keep warm in the oven.

Wipe out the pan very thoroughly. Then, over a high heat, add 2 tablespoons of olive oil. Add the beaten eggs and stir like you would to scramble eggs.

Once the eggs start to set, take the pan away from the heat. Spread the eggs out like you are making a crêpe.

Season with salt and white pepper.

Place the girolles all over the flat omelette. Slice the truffle generously over the top and let the omelette rest in a warm oven for 2 minutes.

Serve with a drizzle of truffled olive oil.

¼ cup olive oil

½ brown onion, finely chopped

2 cloves garlic

200 g girolles (mushrooms), washed and dried

salt and white pepper

2 tablespoons finely chopped flat-leaf parsley

2 tablespoons butter

¼ lemon

8 eggs, beaten

1 × 20 g summer truffle (optional)

truffle oil

FRESH HERBED OMELETTE WITH SMOKED TROUT

Serves 2

¼ cup olive oil

8 eggs, beaten

1 tablespoon finely chopped tarragon

1 teaspoon Provençal thyme, picked

1 tablespoon finely chopped parsley

2 garlic cloves, crushed

½ white onion, finely chopped

2 × 100 g fillets smoked trout, bones removed and broken up

2 Green Zebra tomatoes, finely chopped

salt and white pepper

Pre-heat the oven to 100°C.

Over a high heat, add 2 tablespoons of the olive oil. Add the beaten eggs and stir like you would to scramble eggs.

Once the eggs start to set, take the pan away from the heat. Spread the eggs out like you are making a crêpe. Add the chopped herbs, garlic and onion, sprinkling them all over the flat omelette.

Place the smoked trout and green tomato over the top. Season well with salt and white pepper.

Drizzle with a little more olive oil and let the omelette rest in a warm oven for 2 minutes before serving.

TOMATO, BASIL AND GOAT'S CHEESE OMELETTE

Serves 2

10 golf-ball-size cherry tomatoes, cut in half

4 garlic cloves, crushed

2 sprigs thyme, picked

salt and white pepper

½ cup olive oil

8 eggs, beaten

100 g fresh goats cheese, crumbled

20 fresh basil leaves

Pre-heat the oven to 100°C.

Macerate the tomatoes, garlic, thyme, salt, pepper and half the olive oil in a bowl for 5 minutes.

Place the tomatoes, flesh side up, on an oven tray in the pre-heated oven for 1 hour and slowly roast. (This is optional, but worth it.)

Over a high heat, add 2 tablespoons of olive oil. Add the beaten eggs and stir like you would to scramble eggs.

Once the eggs start to set, take the pan away from the heat. Spread the eggs out like you are making a crêpe.

Add the tomatoes and goat's cheese. Season well with salt and white pepper.

Drizzle with a little more olive oil and let the omelette rest in a warm oven for 2 minutes.

Before serving, rip the basil leaves with your fingers over the top of the omelette.

BOUDIN NOIR AND CAPER OMELETTE

Serves 2

Pre-heat the oven to 100°C.

Over a high heat, add 2 tablespoons of the olive oil. Fry the black pudding for 2 minutes on each side. Add the capers in the last minute of frying.

Season the *boudin* and capers well, and drain on paper towel. Keep warm in the oven.

Wipe the pan clean with paper towel.

Over a high heat, add 2 tablespoons of the olive oil.

Add the beaten eggs and stir like you would to scramble eggs.

Once the eggs start to set, take the pan away from the heat. Spread the eggs out like you are making a crêpe.

Add the black pudding, capers and marjoram over the top. Season well with salt and white pepper.

Drizzle with a little more olive oil and let the omelette rest in a warm oven for 2 minutes before serving

¼ cup olive oil

300 g *boudin noir* (black pudding), sliced and dusted in flour

1 tablespoon drained capers

salt and white pepper

8 eggs, beaten

1 teaspoon picked marjoram leaves

CALISSONS

You will need to start this recipe a day ahead.

Soak the crystallized melon and orange peel in the almond liqueur and orange flour water overnight, then drain. Discard the soaking liquid.

Line a tray of oval-shaped candy moulds with plastic wrap and set aside.

Cream the egg yolks, sugar and ground almonds.

In a separate bowl, beat the heavy cream until soft peaks form. Gently fold the whipped cream and plumped fruits into the egg mixture.

Fill the candy moulds with the nougat batter and freeze until the candies are firm.

Roll them in the confectioner's sugar, if desired, before serving.

55 g crystallized melon, diced

25 g candied orange peel, diced

3 tablespoons almond liqueur

3 tablespoons orange flower water

2 egg yolks

115 g fine granulated sugar

85 g ground almonds

290 ml thick cream

confectioner's sugar

Cheeses of Provence

BANON À LA FEUILLE, the most famous cheese in Provence, is made solely from raw goat's milk and is ripened in chestnut leaves after having been dipped in eau de vie. Banon should be eaten as is, lightly pan-fried, or baked on fresh bread.

Accompanying wine: vin de Cassis or a regional marc.

BROUSSE DU ROVE is a fresh unsalted cheese, once only sold on the streets of Marseille. Its namesake is a small village to the west of the city, and it is claimed that it dates back to a Greek shipwreck more than 2000 years ago.

It is rumoured that the goats from the ship bred with the local goats, creating a tough, dual-purpose breed, whose numbers dropped for some time but are now increasing rapidly thanks to the revival of interest in farmhouse cheeses. This breed thrives on the sparse vegetation of Provence, and each goat provides 1.5 litres of remarkably rich milk for cheese making per day.

The moulded cheese is eaten fresh. It has an extremely short shelf life of only 2–3 days, which means only locals can enjoy this beautiful fresh cheese, which they say is perfectly accompanied by a lavender honey.

There is also a ewe's milk version, known as *fromage frais de corne*, as the cheese was originally moulded inside a sheep's horn.

Accompanying wine: Côtes-de-Provence blanc or rosé.

SAINT-MARCELLIN was originally made from goat's milk, but now tends to be made from cow's milk. A local cheese maker attributes the integrity of the cheese to the white plastic vats (which help control the acidity levels) and the large flat scoops used to move the curds into their draining moulds (which help retain the moisture, flavour and texture of the cheese).

Accompanying wine: Côtes-du-Ventoux, Gigondas, Châteauneuf-du-Pape.

An interesting variant is *Le Pitchou*, an artisanal Saint-Marcellin that is marinated in grape seed oil and *herbes de Provence*.

Accompanying wine: Côtes-du-Rhône.

PICODON DE DIEULEFIT is not strictly a Provençal cheese, being made just across the border in Rhône-Alpes, but its flavours have long been associated with the more-southern region.

Picodon is a goat's milk cheese that has links to both Banon à la Feuille and Saint-Marcellin. It dates back in written accounts to 1320 and is one of the oldest goat's cheeses in this part of France. It was granted AOC status in 1983.

The name comes from the French verb meaning to prick or sting, a traditional reference to its piquant flavour.

Accompanying wine: Rivesaltes.

All of these cheeses, which are closely linked by history, only exist today because of the shared passion and skills of the dedicated group of cheese makers determined to preserve their regional heritage.

If you're in the South of France, don't worry about locating good cheese shops; just head off to the local markets!

Saturday, 24 September

With the end of the month and our time here fast disappear-
ing, the mornings are growing decidedly chilly. While the
days are still warm and sun-drenched, the afternoons seem
to encroach that bit sooner. There is a crispness, too, in the
air now, a bite in the soft breeze that I find quite invigorat-
ing. It's also exciting to see the change in produce at the
markets as the summer yields its last and the hearty winter
product returns.

Apt is our destination again today and we head out early
as I want to nab a clutch of the squab I had spotted on our
last visit. I know that if I'm not at the stall by 10 am they will
be as good as gone.

Naturally, there is the odd upset. Hendrix loses one of
his Thomas the Tank Engine trains mid-journey, requiring a
pit stop to find it. Then we are almost taken out by a tourist
bus while attempting to park. But we finally get there.

I opt to leave the missus, Mum and the kids at a teashop
(direct access to good hot chocolate, and a fantastic biscuit
stall next door should keep them occupied), while Dad,
Liam and I do a quick trip around the already burgeoning
marketplace.

Despite our efforts, there aren't quite enough squab for all of us, so I grab a few quail to make up the numbers. Some handsome Musque de Provence pumpkins and celeriac bulbs join them.

After lunch back at the farmhouse, Madeleine says she is determined to make an upside-down cake for dinner, but is mortified to discover that we forgot to buy any eggs. Our caretaker has abandoned us for the day, so no luck there, and our nearest neighbour is driving a tractor up and down several acres of field. He could probably do without trudging back to his *maison* for a couple of ruddy eggs for a bunch of foreigners.

Lunch has been enjoyed with a couple of terrific wines, so a drive up to Ménerbes isn't on the cards either. It is starting to look like a cake-free day after all, but before our blood sugar levels can breathe a sigh of relief Madeleine points out that we should try the snail and chicken farm directly opposite us. We had been meaning to drop by for the last three weeks, so why not now?

Mum, Dad, Madeleine and the kids make the pilgrimage over. I want to accompany them, but my artichokes are at a precarious stage in their cooking ... that and Arsenal are at a precarious stage of their match against Bolton. Liam stays to help me out—at both!

MADELEINE: The farm is officially closed for midi (the midday break all retailers observe in Provence), but fortunately for us the chickens are being given lunch at just that moment, and the slightly abashed owner (she is wearing pyjamas: they really take their midday break seriously in these parts) kindly agrees to open up and save my dessert.

Saturday, 24 September

A quaint store occupying the front room of the farmhouse offers various permutations of frozen *escargots* (snails), along with chicken, duck and goose fats, salts, pâtés and confitures.

While I blather on in broken French to the chicken-keeper, the kids admire her charges. The chickens are a very pretty breed living free-range, with just a single wire fence separating them from the home. With some funny theatrics, the woman mimes that the fence is electric, so *ne touchez pas*!

The snails live next door beneath numerous wooden slats laid over grass and plants. A low wire has been run around their bed, but no warning has been issued in regard to this. It is inevitable, then, that when Phoenix bends over to investigate these edible snails she cops a mighty zap that gives off an impressive clap and leaves the air humming. It is very low voltage, so no real harm is done, other than to my little girl's pride.

Once the tears subside enough to get a sensible answer out of her, she reports that it didn't hurt too much.

We are all rather mystified as to what the purpose of the fence is. Surely not to keep the snails in? And given it only comes up to Hendrix's kneecap, it wouldn't keep much out. Perhaps it was designed to dissuade the chickens from eating their neighbours, or perhaps to do exactly as it has done: scare the heck out of small children and remind them to keep their little fingers to themselves!

By the time they all get back, it's late in the afternoon and we decide Madeleine's upside-down cake will have to wait until tomorrow.

At least the eggs are superb. Even Dad, who boasts a decent flock of good layers back home, comments on their colour and texture: clear, with firm whites and bright orange yolks.

There is something very humbling about a freshly laid egg, sitting snug in its carton among its mismatched mates, no two exactly alike, each with their own flaws and beauties. There is so much potential hidden within that shell. They are the ultimate chameleon and the perfect foundation for so many meals, friend to protein and vegetable alike, the perfect vehicle for herbs, cheese and seasoning.

Knowing they came from happy hens, living as nature intended and laying only as many as the season and climate allows, with no chemical intervention or interference, is deeply reassuring. The health of the hens is always there in the taste of the eggs.

Saturday, 24 September

EGGS WITH RATATOUILLE

Serves 4

All egg dishes are popular in Provence. This peasant dish is one
I discovered myself and serves very well as a Sunday brunch with
some fresh crusty bread.

The eggs we have been purchasing are extraordinary. The farm
attendant plucks them from the simple nests, which are basically
little holes in the grounds where groups of 6–7 eggs lie. They are so
fresh that the yolks sit tall on top of the translucent whites. I find them
a useful tool in the pleasurable pastime of poaching the perfect shaped
egg. No vinegar is required.

4 cups cooked ratatouille
(see p. 58)

8 free-range eggs

salt and pepper

4 tablespoons olive oil

Pre-heat the oven to 180°C.

In a shallow cast-iron or
earthenware dish, place half
the ratatouille evenly around
the pan, making 8 shallow 'pits'
with the back of a dessertspoon.

Crack the eggs into these 'pits'
and season the top of each egg.
Cover the eggs completely with
the remaining ratatouille.

Place the dish in the oven and
bake for 10 minutes.

Remove from the oven and
drizzle with olive oil.

Serve.

MUSQUE DE PROVENCE PUMPKIN SOUP

2 kg of Musque de
Provence pumpkin

¼ cup olive oil

4 garlic cloves, peeled
and crushed

1 large brown onion,
chopped

500 ml chicken stock

salt and pepper

100 g fresh walnuts,
shelled

¼ bunch chives, finely
chopped

Before visiting this part of the world, I associated pumpkin soup with America, and rightly so. But as September here approaches its peak, I start to notice the fields become more manicured, the grass and vegetation lose their height, and from a distance bright orange dots become noticeable.

Closer inspection fills me with excitement: they are the largest and most texturally challenging pumpkins I have ever touched or witnessed and they fill me with ideas.

Liam and I visit these fields over the next few days, but find the light not right or the pumpkins not quite ripe enough to photograph or pick. In the end, I fight with my excitement and refer back to the simple manuscript on local recipes I discovered at the Lourmarin book fair. It has only '2 recettes' for pumpkin and one is a simple soup.

Please notice that there is no cream anywhere to be seen. Maybe the Americans should take note!

Pre-heat the oven to 160°C.

Cut the pumpkins in half, then de-seed them. Reserve the seeds for toasted pumpkin seeds (below).

Cut the pumpkins into 8 wedges. Place onto a baking tray and drizzle with olive oil. Add the garlic and onion to the tray. Season well with salt and bake for 40 minutes.

In a large saucepan, bring the chicken stock to the boil and then simmer.

Remove the pumpkin from the oven. Let it rest on the bench until okay to touch. Scoop out the flesh from the delicate skin. Do not be too concerned if some skin remains on the flesh. Add to the stock with the onions and garlic. Simmer for a further 10 minutes.

Then, using a hand blender, blend the soup until smooth and season well.

Evenly distribute the fresh walnuts and chives between the bowls. Pour the soup over the top and then finish with a generous drizzle of olive oil.

Serve with bread and butter.

Note: Musque de Provence pumpkins come in various sizes, but one of the most common varieties is small in size, which is perfect for taking the top off and keeping it as a lid.

As a fancy dinner party idea, de-seed the pumpkins, bake whole for 15 minutes at 180°C and then use the hollowed-out pumpkins and lids to serve the soup in.

TOASTED PUMPKIN SEEDS

What better garnish could there be to such a simple soup? But be warned: I have been cooking for more than 20 years and have never perfected the art of toasted pumpkin seeds—not like the ones you get in those alternative laneway bars of Melbourne, where you cannot stop eating them.

The key is patience and making sure they come from a ripe pumpkin. Clean them properly and don't give up until they taste and feel like the greatest pumpkin seeds you have ever tasted.

Oh, and don't be afraid to add different flavours once you have perfected the basic recipe. For example, add some cumin when frying or toasting.

seeds from a ripe pumpkin
salt
garlic powder

Pre-heat the oven to 200°C.

Rinse the seeds in water to remove stringy matter. Blot dry with paper towel.

Place a single layer on a baking sheet (no oil needed). Sprinkle with salt to desired taste and a pinch of garlic powder. Bake for 10–15 minutes.

Flip over and bake for an additional 10 minutes or until the seeds are a light golden brown.

Alternatively, you can try frying the seeds.

Good luck!

SQUAB WITH CELERIAC RÉMOULADE

Serves 6

6 × 600 g squab pigeons

1 lemon, juiced

2 garlic cloves, peeled and crushed

1¾ cups olive oil

2 shallots, finely chopped

¼ cup chopped parsley

1 cup sausage mince

salt and pepper

1 cup fresh breadcrumbs

2 tablespoons red wine vinegar

2 teaspoons sugar

½ lemon

No matter where you are in the world, squab is bloody expensive. The Coustellet *boucherie* has exceptional fresh local birds, reared free-range on the foothills of the Mont Ventoux National Park. They are plump and firm, and the skin is free of any bruising. The only problem is they are 15€ each. To satisfy guests, a good cook will always serve one whole squab per person. The stuffing in this recipe does make it possible, though, to get away with serving half a bird per person.

Place the bowl of a food processor into the freezer.

Remove the livers from the squabs and retain. If there are no livers, substitute with chicken livers.

Rinse the birds and pat dry inside and out. Remove the neck and wishbone of each squab.

Sit the birds in the lemon juice, half the crushed garlic and ¾ cup of the olive oil for a minimum of 90 minutes.

In the very cold bowl of the food processor, add the livers, remaining garlic, chopped shallots, parsley, 2 tablespoons of the oil from the marinade, sausage mince, salt, pepper and breadcrumbs. Pulse until combined. Season well.

Place the stuffing inside the cavity of each squab.

Set up the rôtissiere on a barbecue.

Place the metal skewer of the motorized rôtisserie through the centre of each bird, pushing it onto the skewer. Roast for 35 minutes, continuously basting with the marinade. If you don't have a barbecue with a rôtisserie (the preferred method of cooking), roast the squabs in a 180°C oven for 18 minutes, basting regularly.

Rest the squabs on a plate for 5 minutes. Drain any juices from the resting plate into a bowl.

Add the red wine vinegar, sugar, a squeeze of lemon juice and the remaining cup of olive oil to the bowl with the juices. Whisk together and serve spooned over a whole squab with a generous serve of celeriac rémoulade (see below).

CELERIAC RÉMOULADE

Serves 6 as a main garnish

I include celeriac rémoulade in this study of modern Provençal food, having learnt that rémoulade is a derivative of aioli sauce.

I have no idea if I am going to offend the French, but I'm declaring right here and now that vegetable rémoulade is not from Lyon. It's Provençal!

Every *boucherie* and small store sells pre-made celeriac rémoulade and it's delicious. It goes so well with any saucy, salty Provençal braise like *daube*, rabbit or chicken.

1 small celeriac, julienned
to the shape of matchsticks

1 small onion, finely
chopped

1 apple, julienned

6 tablespoons garlic
mayonnaise

salt and pepper

Combine all the ingredients in
a large bowl and mix well.

Serve.

Every garden in the Luberon seems to have a quince tree.
It originated in Asia, but after I visited Istanbul I've tended
to associate the quince and its products with Turkey.
I didn't think for a second when planning this book that
the quince would add so much colour to the sides of so
many country roads.

I have also come to appreciate the smell they give off
in the late afternoon as the sun penetrates their flesh.
It makes my jogs a pleasure.

Quinces are too hard, astringent and sour to eat raw
unless 'bletted' (softened by the early frosts). They then
start to break down on the tree and are eaten by farmers
in the late morning.

I have learnt to make jelly and quince purées with
them, which I use in soufflés and with game meats. The
flesh of the fruit turns red after a long cooking time.

The very strong perfume means they can be added in
small quantities to apple recipes to enhance the flavour.
The term 'marmalade', originally meaning a quince purée

used for adding to sauces, is derived from *marmelo*, the Portuguese word for quince. That adds even more mystery as to why this fruit has implanted itself into the culture of the Luberon.

Madeleine finally gets to bake her upside-down quince cake, while I try a universal recipe for poached quinces.

Those eggs from across the road give Madeleine's cake mix a glossy, golden hue and the cake comes up a treat. And to make up for Phoenix's war wounds, suffered yesterday in the brave line of duty, she scores two serves!

SHANNON'S POACHED QUINCES

Place all the ingredients, including the cores and the vanilla pods and seeds, together in a Le Creuset–type casserole dish with a lid. Bring to the boil, then turn heat down to a simmer and cook for 2 hours.

Always keep the seeds with the quince whilst cooking. They are very high in pectin and this is a natural gelatine that will help to set any purées or jams.

Reserve the poaching juices and chill in the fridge before using.

3–4 quinces, washed and cut in half (or cored and sliced lengthways, about 5 cm thick, for the upside-down cake)

2 star anise

1 teaspoon crushed white peppercorns

1 vanilla pod, halved and seeded

2 cups water or any leftover sweet wine

1 cup brown sugar

1 lemon, juiced and zested

Wine

Try a sparkling wine, or even cider mixed with quince purée. It makes a great afternoon cocktail.

MADELEINE'S UPSIDE-DOWN QUINCE CAKE

¾ cup butter

½ cup brown sugar

½ cup water

1 quantity Shannon's
poached quinces
(see p. 179)

1 cup sugar

2 eggs, separated

1 vanilla pod,
halved and seeded

1½ cup plain flour

2 teaspoons baking
powder

pinch salt

½ cup milk

Place ¼ cup butter, brown sugar and water in a small saucepan, and boil until the sugar dissolves.

Over a medium heat, boil the caramel until the colour changes into a light brown. Remove and let cool.

Pre-heat the oven to 180°C.

Grease and line the base of a 24-cm round cake tin.

Spread the prepared caramel over the base of the tin and lay poached quince on top.

Cream the remaining butter and sugar. Beat in the egg yolks and vanilla seeds.

Alternating with additions of the milk, gradually sift in the flour and baking powder, and add the salt.

Whip the egg whites until soft peaks form, and fold gently through the cake mixture.

Pour the mixture over the quinces. Bake for 40–45 minutes.

While the cake is baking, reduce the reserved poaching juices by half, until dark and viscous.

When baked, allow the cake to cool for 5 minutes in the tin.

Turn out directly onto a serving plate. Glaze generously with reduced juices.

Note: By poaching the quinces with the cores intact, the seeds release pectin into the juices. When reduced down and spread over the cake, the glaze sets as a soft, shiny jelly thanks to the natural gelatine created by the poaching process.

I have been up since 4.30 am. I have to drop brother Liam back at the TGV station in Avignon.

Liam has been blown away by the simplicity of life over here, how all the shops close in the afternoon, and the locals take the time to sit down and eat lunch properly with a glass of red wine—no matter if they are at work or not! It seems like no one is on the conveyor belt of life here. They let the seasons shape their daily lives and fill them with the simple but exciting pleasures that we city dwellers crave yet abuse.

Driving back from Avignon along the N900, I stop at the *boulangerie* in Coustellet and watch the baker working his ass off. I buy baguettes, and brioche buns that have been glazed with fondant icing and are still warm.

It is a nice feeling getting back to the house in the just-broken light with warm baked goods for breakfast. The kids get all excited and fight over whose brioche is bigger. Some things in life don't change no matter where you are.

A late lunch—made up of leftover cheese and baguettes with a rosé made from the grapes in the backyard—makes me tired. I always refuse to take a nap in the afternoons—it just doesn't feel right—so I decide instead to test out my Nike/iPod running sensor. It fits into my Nike runners and is the size of a 10-cent piece. Somehow it talks to my iPod and tells me exactly how many kilometres I have run, the time it has taken and how many calories I have burned up. What can I say? It's the modern world!

I run the 10.3 kilometres in 43 minutes. This includes a three-minute stop under my favourite fig tree to snack on a couple of the energising figs. I have never tasted figs like these: it's like eating little pots of fig-flavoured honey. Maybe it's the view of the village in the background, but since my first day here, when I jogged up the back road to Ménerbes, I have been obsessed by this fig tree and its fruit.

Back home, and after the adrenalin from the run has faded away, I become aware how empty the place has become without Liam. This is despite the presence of Madeleine, my parents and three young children!

I decide to cheer us all up with my favourite culinary discovery of the trip: turkey leg and pearl barley!

If I were to classify one category of food that is expensive in Provence, it would have to be meat. It's at least three times as expensive as it is in Australia.

One meat that defies this rule is turkey. At 8€ a kilo, it's a steal. Everybody in this part of the world consumes it regularly and I don't think price has much to do with it. The flavour, yield and flexibility have everything to do with it. One leg can weigh as much as a kilo and half. It can be roasted, braised or de-boned, sliced and pan-fried.

The cèpes season is in full swing and, as I have started to crave dried cèpes, I have picked up 10 g of house-dried cèpes from the butcher, along with some pearl barley. The butcher tells me pearl barley is the food that feeds the soul of Provence. It's also the only food farmers share with their livestock.

BRAISED TURKEY LEG (CUISSE DE DINDE) WITH PEARL BARLEY

Serves 4

1 × 1 kg turkey leg

10 g dried cèpes

3 bay leaves

200 g dried pearl barley, pre-soaked for 4 hours

3 shallots, finely chopped

1 cup sweet wine or sherry

1 litre chicken stock or water

½ cup olive oil

2 tablespoons shallot vinegar (see p. 97)

2 tablespoons parsley, chopped

1 teaspoon chopped lemon thyme

salt and pepper

Before you start cooking, soak the pearl barley for at least 4 hours.

Pre-heat the oven to 140°C.

In a large casserole dish, place the turkey leg, cèpes, bay leaves, pearl barley, shallots, sherry, and stock or water. Season well.

Over a high heat, bring to the boil.

Place the lid on tightly and then put into the oven for 3 hours.

Remove the turkey leg from the pearl barley and divide up the meat into 4 even portions. Keep warm.

Place the casserole dish with the pearl barley onto a stove over a low heat. Stir in the olive oil and vinegar (to taste, not all at once), and the chopped herbs. Taste and season well. The texture of the barley should be the consistency of a wet risotto.

Ladle the barley onto each plate and place a piece of turkey meat on top. Serve immediately with a side of Green Beans with Pimentée Purée.

GREEN BEANS WITH PIMENTÉE PURÉE, SERVED COLD

Serves 4

500 g topped baby green beans (*haricots verts*)

2 garlic cloves, crushed

1 brown onion, finely chopped

1 cup pimentée sauce (see p. 83)

¼ cup olive oil

salt and pepper

The *haricots verts* (green beans) in the local markets are beautiful and, no, they are not imported from Kenya. They are all stacked beautifully in neat rows and packed in wooden boxes. Cooking them takes a matter of seconds rather than minutes, retaining the vibrant colour and crunchiness, as well as their beautiful herbaceous flavour.

I could list a few dozen serving suggestions, but the recipe below is a true representation of the early autumn, when there is vibrant colour in all the dishes on the table.

Blanch the beans for 4 minutes in boiling salted water. Drain well.

Whilst the beans are still hot, mix all the remaining ingredients in a bowl with a whisk.

Add the green beans to the dressing and season well.

Let the dressed beans macerate for 30–60 minutes before serving.

Wine

M. Chapoutier is a major producer of the Northern Rhône, but with excellent wines from Southern Rhône as well, and such far-flung places as Australia! Try the Chapoutier Luberon or Côtes-de-Roussillon for an excellent regional match.

Day
25

Tuesday, 27 September

The feeling of emptiness continues here and the wind has picked up. The silence of the birds and insects, which allows us to hear the trees wallow and rustle, makes me feel like everyone has packed up and moved on.

I try to cheer myself up—this time with a variety of salads and courgette flowers for lunch, and cabbage Provençal for dinner.

Food and the innocence of the children having a really great time are the only two things that make the depressive atmosphere fade.

COURGETTE BEIGNETS

Makes 10 beignets

10 courgette flowers

BATTER
200 g plain flour
200 ml beer

RATATOUILLE FILLING
ratatouille (see p. 58)

SMOKED HAM, SAGE AND BROUSSE DU ROVE FILLING
100 g ham, roughly chopped
2 sprigs sage, picked and chopped
100 g Brousse du Rove, diced
salt and pepper

There are two types of courgette flowers: the female, which has the immature 'zucchini' attached; and the male, which just has the stem attached. Both taste the same, but I prefer the male: the flowers are slightly larger and the stems cook quickly. This enables the delicate flowers to be served at their optimum quality.

Modern cookery really only showcases courgette flowers as *beignets* (battered and fried). The perfect batter for a courgette flower is one that is very light.

The *beignets* can be made without a filling, but some suggestions for filling the courgette flowers are also included. Remember less is more! Overfilling the flowers will result in leakage, ruining the oil and lowering the temperature—thus, soggy batter.

For the batter, whisk the flour and beer until smooth. If you have a cream charge syphon gun, place the batter into the canister, seal tightly, charge with 2 bulbs and shake well.

For courgette beignets with ratatouille, fill each flower with 1 dessertspoon of the ratatouille.

For courgette *beignets* with smoked ham, sage and Brousse du Rove, mix together the ingredients and season with salt and pepper.

Use 1 dessertspoon of mix to fill each flower.

To complete the b*eignets*, pre-heat 1 litre of good olive oil to 170°C.

Place the courgettes (filled or unfilled) into a bowl and squeeze or spoon over a little of the batter. Coat evenly, using your fingertips, and place into the boiling oil. Cook for 2 minutes or until golden.

Drain onto paper towel and season well.

Serve.

COCO BEAN SALAD

Serves 4

400 g cooked *haricots blanc* (white beans)
1 onion, finely diced
1 red bell pepper, roasted, then finely chopped
1 cup mature rocket leaves, roughly chopped to the same size as a single bean
1 lemon, zested and juiced
½ cup olive oil
salt and pepper

The term 'coco bean' is used a lot to describe what I call a dried *haricot blanc*. In the markets, a lot of the full-time stalls sell the cooked beans already prepared in the jar ready for lunch. I asked one of the store holders for their recipe. It pairs really well with some fresh crab meat and rouille.

Combine all the ingredients together and season well. Serve at room temperature.

COURGETTE CRÊPES

Makes 8 crêpes

Another good idea to try one day is courgette crêpes. They work a treat.

CRÊPE BATTER
2 large eggs, beaten

½ cup plain flour

¾ cup milk

COURGETTE MIX
2 medium courgettes, julienned into the shape of matchsticks

2 tablespoons shallot vinegar (see p. 97)

8 courgette flowers, roughly chopped

1 tablespoon tarragon, finely chopped

4 tablespoons grated Emmenthal

2 tablespoons olive oil

salt and pepper

TO COMPLETE
¼ cup olive oil

For the crêpe batter, in a food processor or with a whisk, combine the eggs and flour until the mixture is smooth. Add the milk gradually, whisking or by pulsing between each addition, to make a smooth batter. It should resemble light cream.

Transfer the crêpe batter into a pouring jug. This will make it easier to pour the batter into the pan.

Leave the batter to rest for 30 minutes before using.

For the courgette mix, combine all the ingredients well and season. Use immediately to prevent the courgettes from bleeding and becoming soggy.

To complete, using a scrunched-up piece of paper towel and a generous amount of olive oil, lightly grease a heavy-based, non-stick pan with a diameter of at least 20 cm. Place the pan over a medium heat.

When the pan starts to lightly smoke, pour in about 2 tablespoons of batter and quickly swirl the pan to produce a crêpe with a diameter of about 18 cm. If you find that the batter is a little too thick to produce a thin, even crêpe, add a dash of extra milk to the batter.

Sprinkle 1 tablespoon of the courgette mixture evenly over the crêpe while the batter is still wet. This timing is important as the courgette needs to set into the batter.

Cook until the top of the crêpe loses its shiny, wet appearance and the underside is lightly browned. Loosen the edges of the crêpe with a palate knife or spatula.

Flip the crêpe and cook the other side until it has begun to colour. This will take half the time as the first side.

Remove the cooked crêpe from the pan and place on a lightly greased plate. Spoon one more tablespoon of the courgette mix evenly over the cooked crêpe and keep in a warm oven.

Repeat the same process for all 8 crêpes.

Before serving, fold the crêpes into quarters and serve 2 crispy, golden crêpes per person.

Do not store the crêpes. Serve immediately!

CABBAGE PROVENÇAL

Serves 4

Given the history of cabbage in this region, its traditional non-association with Provence actually annoys me a fair bit. The pre–16th century archival facts, housed in Avignon, speak for themselves.

It was cabbages, goat and pork that kept the locals from starving. There were no carrots or courgette fields, while tomatoes were rare and only for the privileged. Locals could not simply walk into a neighbour's vineyard and take a bunch of grapes!

Provence was its own state, one that had practical hardships, and its food was shaped around this: salted fish, salted meats, vegetables pickled in vinegars, and short seasons of limited fresh vegetables.

Cabbage was the exception to this: easy to grow, a good shelf life and available 9 months of the year. (In the dead of winter they simply do not grow.)

Cabbages are everywhere and all the local people I speak with have a favourite recipe. They all seem to add meat in some form. This makes it a complete meal.

1 smooth green cabbage (not the Savoy variety), chopped

2 brown onions, finely diced

4 garlic cloves, finely crushed

½ cup olive oil, and extra for serving

4 Merguez sausages, cut up

4 large Beefsteak tomatoes, placed in a food processor and blended

salt and pepper

¼ cup flat-leaf parsley, chopped

Pre-heat the oven to 160°C.

In a large oven-proof pot over a medium heat, cook the chopped cabbage, onions and garlic with the olive oil.

Add the sausages and tomatoes. Bring to the boil and season well.

Cover the pot tightly with a lid and place in the oven for 1 hour.

Serve drizzled with more olive oil and fresh chopped parsley.

Wednesday, 28 September

All the markets are now overflowing with Globe artichokes.

I have never really associated France with the heart of an artichoke and its amazing repertoire of dishes, but dig below the surface and you find the Globe artichoke is an important part of Provençal cuisine.

The first evidence of their use is in the *bibliothèque* of Avignon, where the records show the official town gardens were planted with them both as ornaments and for harvest. The earliest recipes show they were roasted whole with olive oil, then picked with the hands at the table to accompany roast meats. Originating along the African Mediterranean coast, where they still grow wild, artichokes were introduced to the Romans by the Greeks. That trail leads us to Provence.

Today's Provençal recipes have embraced the 'religious'–like procedures involved in the preparation of an artichoke, but the results are rewarding. Once the method of peeling and turning is mastered, smaller-sized artichokes can be chosen. These have the added bonus of tender stems. Peeling them will reveal the same flesh as the heart.

Keep in mind artichokes are in the top category for nutritional and medicinal value, and very high in antioxidants, vitamins and minerals. But do not confuse Globe artichokes and Jerusalem artichokes, which are tubers. They have opposing harvesting seasons, the Globe appearing towards the end of summer and early autumn, and the Jerusalem in the middle of winter.

With no rules on the size of the artichokes in the markets, just simple rubber bands around 4–5 heads, I'm amazed at their popularity and all the shopping bags I see filled with them.

I find it hard to imagine that in Australia the public would take the time to prepare an artichoke properly or see the beauty in a well-prepared heart. There really is no shortcut to the preparation of an artichoke. It takes the art of a chef to really achieve the perfect bell shape of a turned artichoke. Here, in the markets, everybody seems to be a chef!

Artichokes are prone to very rapid oxidization. Using lemon juice is a good preventative measure, but the biggest mistake of even the world's best chefs is to overuse this acid in the preparation. The result is a permanent pickled taste to the artichoke. What's the point?

Another terrible practice is to store raw artichokes in water and acid. This dilutes the flavour, changes the texture, and releases valuable antioxidants and vitamins into the water.

My solution to all these problems is to follow the recipe below for all Globe artichoke preparation.

ARTICHOKE BARIGOULE

Makes 6

1 lemon, juiced

½ cup shallot vinegar (see p. 97)

8 large artichokes

½ cup extra virgin olive oil, and extra for serving

1 large brown onion, thinly sliced across the grain

5 small carrots, peeled and thinly sliced

5 garlic cloves, peeled and crushed

4 fresh bay leaves

5 thyme sprigs

5 sprigs fresh coriander seeds and their stems

350 ml white wine

2 oranges, juiced

leftover juice from 1 jar gherkins or capers

500 ml chicken stock or a Knorr stock cube in 500 ml water

salt and pepper

In a large bowl, put 1 tablespoon of the lemon juice and half the shallot vinegar.

Using a sharp serrated knife, remove the stems then halve the artichokes crosswise. Discard the tops.

Working with 1 artichoke at a time, pull off the outer green leaves until you start to struggle with pulling the leaves away (refer to photos on p. 197).

Using a sharp utility knife and starting at the base, trim and turn the artichoke. Continue to dip the artichoke into the vinegar and lemon juice. This will prevent the oxidization and rapid discolouration of the flesh.

I would best describe the shape of the eventual 'turned' artichoke as a bell. Remember to carefully turn with the motto 'less is more'. It's easy for a novice to turn an artichoke into a scraggly mess, and the end result is 'Artichokes are a fuss about nothing!'

Repeat with the remaining artichokes, placing each turned artichoke in the vinegar and lemon juice when it's finished

In a large pot, heat the olive oil over a medium-to-high heat.

Add the onion and carrots, and cook over moderate heat, stirring until softened but not browned—about 4 minutes.

Add the garlic, bay leaves, thyme and coriander seeds and stems, and bring to the boil.

Add the wine, orange juice, remaining lemon juice, gherkin or caper juice, remaining vinegar and stock. Bring to a boil over a high heat.

Remove the turned artichokes from the vinegar and lemon juice and place in the pot. Do not add the juices from the preparation: they will be bitter in taste. Bring to the boil and then turn down to a simmer.

Cover with a *cartouche* (circle of paper) and cook the artichokes for 30 minutes, before removing from the heat. Test the artichokes with a knife.

Remove the artichokes from the liquor—this will make a great broth—and place onto some paper towel to drain.

Proceed, while the artichokes are still warm, to pull the purple petals from the choke. Retain the petals as a garnish.

Once down to the choke, pull the choke out in pieces with your fingers. If the artichokes are cooked, this step will be easy.

If not using the artichokes immediately, keep them refrigerated in the *barigoule* broth.

When serving, cut each artichoke into 6 pieces (this may depend on the size).

Spoon the pieces into warm bowls, drizzle with a little olive oil, garnish with artichoke petals and serve.

Note: Before preparing any other food, be sure to carefully wash your hands as they will otherwise impart a bitter taste to whatever you are making.

STUFFED ARTICHOKES WITH RATATOUILLE

Makes 4

Pre-heat the oven to 140°C.

Place the artichokes with the hollow side up on an oven tray. Season well and drizzle a little olive oil on them.

Spoon in the ratatouille until the whole artichoke is filled.

Place in the oven and bake for 20 minutes. Drizzle with a little more olive oil and serve.

I recommend serving with roasted pigeon or quail (see pp. 72 and 174).

4 large turned and cooked artichokes

salt and pepper

olive oil

8 tablespoons ratatouille (see p. 58)

Day 27

Thursday, 29 September

The weather is stunning, with hardly any wind and not a
cloud in the sky. The air temperature I imagine is about 28°C.

There are no markets today. It's the end of the season and
the small markets have closed for the year. Most will return
in the first week of May.

I head to our local *boucherie* and pick up some pieces
of the lamb saddle that no one wants. They are the pieces
that connect the back to the rump. I find these cuts great for
roasting and braising. I'll serve them with preserved lemons.

I have a feeling the butcher thinks I'm a gay crime novelist
researching a new book. In the time between introducing
myself to him and now, he still hasn't realized that all the
questions I have asked are related to a cookbook and
of general interest to a chef.

Today he asks me: 'Your chef character in the book, does
he die in the end?'

I have no idea what to say, so I reply: 'Yes, but of happiness!'

He gives me a strange look and continues to chop away.

This is a great little shop and I have built a relationship with this man. A butcher in the Luberon is like the local doctor. He fixes problems by way of happiness in the stomach. He sells all sorts of foodstuffs, not only fresh meat, but preserved meats, potted terrines, parfaits, cooked casseroles, the works. It is all beautifully presented.

One of the daily pleasures I will really miss when I get back to Australia is my visit to one of the two local butcher shops in Ménerbes and Coustellet.

PRESERVED LEMONS

On our second day in the Luberon, I picked up some very small, greenish lemons. I decided at the time to preserve them. Because of their size, I had enough time.

I have always been intrigued by how fancy providores and even *boucheries* are able to secure those pretty little lemons tightly bottled in the jars. They make great gifts.

At the end of the lemon season they appear as immature lemons, but with a large amount of flesh. If you do come across these sorts of lemons, there may be insufficient acid in them to successfully pickle them, so simply add extra lemon juice to the jar.

Always discard the salty bitter flesh and just use the skin in all sorts of dishes, from Indian to Moroccan.

This recipe is a great snapshot of what rural Provence is today. Every small-town greengrocer has a stock of preserved lemons. It's terrible to read all this nonsense about how people's eating habits are ruined today. It is compete rubbish. One must travel to the Luberon and stay a little while before making such rash, attention-seeking assessments.

8 small lemons, from towards the end of the season

200 g sea salt

3 star anise

4 bay leaves

Scrub the lemons well to remove any dirt or even wax in some cases.

Cut the bottom off each lemon—about 4–5 mm—so it can stand up. Make a 2–3 cm cross in the flat part of the lemon.

Pack the inside of the lemons with sea salt, pushing it in through the slit. Get the salt in as far as you can without damaging the look of the lemons.

Place the lemons in a suitable preserving jar, packing each lemon on the outside with salt and firmly pushing as many as you can into the jar.

Randomly place the star anise and bay leaves inside the jar. Keep in the fridge for 7–8 weeks before using.

Once opened, use within 18 months.

LAMB CASSOULET WITH PRESERVED LEMON, AND AN OLIVE OIL AND POTATO PURÉE

Makes 4

1 kg lamb saddle pieces on the bone (the cut—normally 200 g pieces—is called *selle* in *boucheries*)

3 shallots, finely chopped

2 tablespoons olive oil

4 garlic cloves, crushed

1 tablespoon pickled capers

2 anchovies, crushed

10 coriander seeds, finely crushed

½ bottle white or rosé wine

4 Beefsteak tomatoes, puréed

2 preserved lemons, flesh discarded, pith finely diced

2 sprigs rosemary, picked and finely chopped

salt and pepper

Trim the lamb pieces of all the fat. Season well and leave to the side.

Pre-heat the oven to 140°C.

Heat a large casserole dish over a medium heat. Sweat off the shallots in the olive oil. Add the garlic, capers, anchovies and coriander seeds. Cook for 1 minute.

Add the wine and boil for 2 minutes.

Then add the tomato purée and preserved lemon. Season well and place in the oven for 2 hours, sealed firmly.

Once the meat is tender and falling off the bone, add the rosemary and cook in the oven for a further 10 minutes.

Serve with olive oil and potato purée (see below), and green beans (without the pimentée sauce). Find the finest and smallest *haricots verts* available.

OLIVE OIL AND POTATO PURÉE

Makes 4

4 large starchy potatoes, peeled

8 garlic cloves, peeled

salt

1 cup olive oil

A little tip for this recipe: use enough olive oil to make the potatoes light and buttery. The amount of olive oil that can be successfully emulsified into the starch depends on the variety of potato being used. The more the better, I say.

Don't confuse this recipe with my aioli, which is a dip. Here the potato replaces the egg yolk as the emulsifier.

Cook the potatoes and the garlic cloves in boiling salted water until the potatoes are tender. Drain well.

Place the potatoes and garlic into a food processor and blend.

Add the olive oil a third at a time so it does not split. Blend until smooth and re-season.

Serve.

Friday, 30 September

It's 5:30 am and I am loading the Q7 wagon we have called our own for the past 28 days. It is time to leave the Luberon.

I always have a sense of anxiety when packing up a car in the cold before dawn. Maybe it's the thought of not knowing what the day will bring. This unease usually brings with it a burst of dogged determination to look forward and plan my journey towards even greater financial success, so that one day I will have the freedom to find again the strong sense of happiness and belonging that I have been experiencing here.

Part of that plan will involve me reconsidering my work schedule and thinking about moving here for half the year— or even a month. I could buy an old farmhouse at very little cost, but cost is not the issue. Courage is.

I have always faced challenges with the knowledge that hard work means no ups and downs, no great happiness, no great sadness, just a willingness to get through. That old motto of 'The harder you work, the luckier you get' has always been with me. The only problem is hard work is very distracting and you can fail to recognize good luck when it arrives.

However, I get the sense that the past 28 days of great food, time spent with my wonderful family and a little wine have finally led me towards the path of new understanding. Thank you, Provence.

I will miss the 10-kilometre round jogs up to Ménerbes, picking up a glass of cold beer at the news agency at the top of the village and then trying to jog home with fresh bread under my arm, along the way stopping to pull a sun-warmed fig off the tree where they taste of honey. Those figs have been my Provençal energy bars.

I will miss the clean air. It honestly smells like the old Westmeadows, my childhood home, as it used to be before the Cleanaway landfill moved in, the airport grew and streets became packed with V8 Fords.

The subtle aromas of fresh grass, old dried grass, toasted sage and dried lavender tell me to stop and 'Take the time to smile and feel.'

For the first time, I have really started to understand my children, watching them crack walnuts found fallen to the ground, with a utensil as simple as a rock on a concrete step and making an awful mess. I remember telling my youngest, Xascha, that she couldn't eat the black half-decomposed skin and shell, even though to her it probably tasted like refined mud!

In the Luberon, I actually had the time to listen to them tell stories with so much excitement and based on something as simple as observing a bumble bee. Their hand signals, smiles, running, and eating with their fingers as a sign of 'God, that tasted good' now mean so much to me.

As I continue to pack up the car, I wonder too about the food of Provence. Is it really the star of French cuisine?

Of course it is. Who could argue with an area so diverse and produce so varying that it gave birth to bouillabaisse, pistou, pissaladière, tapenade, tartines and everything *à la Provençale*?

Cooking today is about performing a confirmation of beautiful ingredients, rather than manhandling and bruising them to inflate one's ego and appear a 'super-hot' chef.

It's now easier than ever to experience the pleasure that comes from transforming a chicken that already tastes good into a truly great meal. I have started to cook with my eyes closed, and my sense of smell and feel have become my GPS.

It isn't so much that I learnt new techniques, but that I began to celebrate tradition and history more. And history tells me to be patient.

I know that my communication with my chefs will never change, but it certainly will with my suppliers. They are the chefs of the paddock.

In many ways, this Luberon trip was a homecoming for me, bringing me back in touch with so much of what I loved here as a young apprentice. For every time I come to France I feel rejuvenated and excited.

Sure I am sad to be leaving, and once again battle the demands of a busy work life with spending more time with Madeleine and the children, but I feel as if I can become much better at all I do.

These 28 days in the Luberon have been a revelation and I can't wait to put into practice all that I have learnt. Travel both broadens the mind and narrows the focus. What I have to do now is concentrate on my family and on producing great food.

I know now I am the luckiest man in the world.

HELPFUL INFORMATION

THE GOLDEN TRIANGLE

The Golden Triangle is a term that originates from the 1970s, when journalists began to write up the particularly picturesque area of the Luberon along the Calavon River, north of the mountains of the Petit Luberon.

The Triangle is generally agreed to incorporate the villages of Gordes and Roussillon to the north, and Ménerbes, Lacoste and Bonnieux to the south, with Goult, Oppède and Oppède-le-Vieux in the middle.

It can get a little puzzling trying to work out which of these villages to visit, so here is a snapshot of what I like most about the main villages of The Golden Triangle.

I have added a few hotel and restaurant suggestions, which have been compiled with some help from my mate Scott, who started visiting the Luberon before I was born!

MIEL
Produits de
la ruche
LAVANDIN
TRUFFES

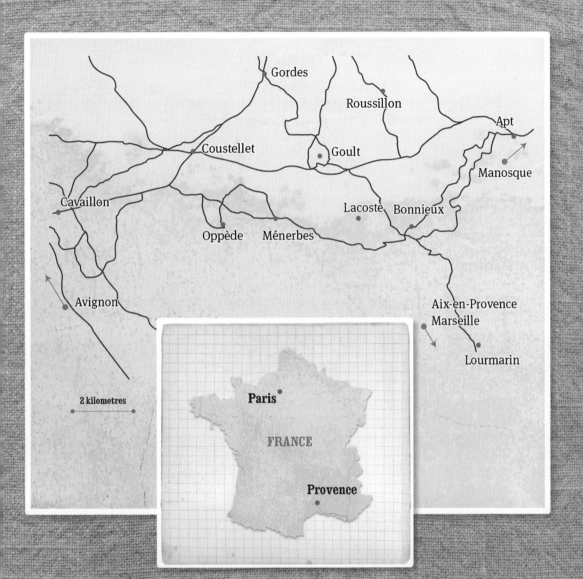

Gordes

Roussillon

Apt

Coustellet

Goult

Manosque

Cavaillon

Lacoste

Bonnieux

Oppède

Ménerbes

Avignon

Aix-en-Provence
Marseille

Lourmarin

2 kilometres

Paris

FRANCE

Provence

THE GOLDEN TRIANGLE

BONNIEUX

Bonnieux is a hill village on the border between the Petit and Grand Luberon. It is famed for its cedar forest, which is stocked full of cèpes in the autumn. Drive through the town in the direction of Lourmarin and you will soon pick up a sign to the forest (Fôret des Cèdres), approximately 2 kilometres from the centre of the village.

This is my favourite of all the old towns in the Luberon. It partly has something to do with sitting in chef Edouard Loubet's garden at La Bastide de Capelongue, sipping a lemon verbena and vodka cocktail and watching the sun set over Lacoste and Mont Ventoux in the background. It's very special.

The town's bread museum is well worth a visit. You will discover the significance of the area in the production of grain, with records showing that the local population of Goults traded grain with the Romans. Walking through a bread museum is not something that may excite most people on a holiday to France, but I came away with a sense of gratitude that a village had gone to so much trouble to construct such a beautiful museum on a subject we should all know more about.

There is also a great French movie memorabilia shop next door that has some quirky posters and many collectors' items. The owner is not someone you would expect to find in a small country town in the middle of nowhere.

The 88-step walk to the top of the town takes some fitness. I motivated myself by repeating the words 'rosé', 'vodka' and 'beer', in no particular order, over and over again on the way up. I found the walk so much easier.

The Friday market is okay, but not my favourite. It does have some good little food stalls, but most of the market is taken up with arts-and-crafts stalls. They are a waste of money, and no good with a 3- and a 6-year-old in tow who naturally want everything they see and more.

Restaurants are plentiful in the town, but most are ordinary. I would say it is best to use them as a pit stop for a cold beer or wine.

L'Arome is not bad. A friendly couple own it and it has a simple, short menu with a nice setting: you feel like you are sitting in a wine cellar.

La Bastide de Capelongue, just outside the village, is a world-class country hotel, while the food at the two-star restaurant is very good and sometimes outstanding. The ambiance and setting are stunning, and the accommodation excellent, with a great country feel.

I recommend staying in the main house, where breakfast is a real treat on a warm morning, sitting on the terraced gardens that look down on the village of Bonnieux, which looks like it's clinging to the side of the hill, with cherry orchards and vineyards below. Quite magical. One word of advice: when visiting the restaurant, order à la carte and dine at lunch time. The atmosphere is more local and upbeat.

LUXURY RESTAURANT-HOTEL

La Bastide de Capelongue

Chef: Edouard Loubet
Domaine de Capelongue
Les Claparèdes,
2 km on the chemin des Cabannes
04 90 75 89 78
capelongue.com
Michelin: ★★
GaultMillau: ♟♟♟♟
Menu: 58 (weekday lunch)/140/190€
À la carte: 130–180€
Hotel rating: 4★+
Rooms: 18
Suites: 9
Single: 160–220€
Double: 190–380€
Breakfast: 22€
Edouard Loubet's magnificent domain,
with food to match. If the soufflé
flavoured with the sap of cedar trees
is on the menu, don't miss it!

RESTAURANTS

L'Arôme

Chef: Jean-Michel Pagès
2 rue Lucien-Blanc
04 90 75 88 62
larome-restaurant.com
GaultMillau: ♟
Menu: 29/38€
À la carte: 45–70€
A simple and friendly restaurant.

Le Fournil

Chef: Guy Malbec
5 place Carnot
04 90 75 83 62
lefournil-bonnieux.com
Menu: 27 (lunch)/55€
À la carte: 27–55€
An always-packed restaurant (you must
book), part of which is located inside
a troglodytic cave.

HOTEL

Le Clos du Buis

rue Victor Hugo
04 90 75 88 48
leclosdubuis.fr
Rating: 3★
Rooms: 8
Single: 102–132€
Double: 102–132€
Breakfast: included in room rate
A charming hotel in the lower part of
Bonnieux, with delicious breakfasts
(especially the homemade tarts).

RESTAURANT (NEARBY)

Auberge de la Loube

Chef: Maurice Leporati
Buoux, 8 km east on the D232 ns D113
04 90 74 19 58
no website ♟
GaultMillau: ♟
Menu: 31/34€
À la carte: 40€
Made famous by *A Year in Provence*.

GORDES

Facing the Luberon, Gordes is certainly the most spectacular village I have seen. The valley below consists of vineyards and meticulously manicured farming land in a pallet of Van Gough–like colours. It creates the setting for a fun and atmospheric village. I prefer entering the village from Roussillon rather than the Goult side. Driving past many farms-turned-luxury homes and the odd boutique hotel builds the anticipation as you join the main road into the village. Parking is always a nightmare. My advice is to head to the main car park on the bend before the final hill up to Gordes.

This town is pretty well closed on Mondays. The market is every Tuesday and starts around 9 am. If you decide to visit on a market day, arrive early—anytime before 9.30 am.

The cafés in Gordes are all situated in places with great views. Two of my favourites are the crêperie, opposite the post office, and the bar on the right-hand side with a very small terrace. Be careful in Gordes when it comes to ATM machines: there is only one in the whole town and the queue can be horrendous.

My favourite vegetable and providore shop is in Gordes. It is very close to the crêperie and stocks only locally grown fruits and vegetables, plus a small selection of vinegars, oils and wines. It has this very old-world feel that is polished off beautifully with a friendly smile.

The only two *boulangeries* in the town are very special. Both have great croissants and speciality cakes, such as the *tarte tropézienne*, and beautiful bread. Of all the bakeries in the Luberon, both these make my Top Five (see p. 67).

The market itself is very arts and crafty, but it brings with it atmosphere and seems to attract a local crowd.

Gordes gets a cool breeze once September hits, so always pack a light sweater if visiting in the early morning.

LUXURY RESTAURANT-HOTELS

Les Bories & Spa

Chef: Pascal Ginoux
2 km along the route de l'Abbaye de Sénanque
04 90 72 00 51
hotellesbories.com
Michelin: ★
GaultMillau: ♨♨
Menu: 58 (weekday lunch)/140/190€
À la carte: 130–180€
Hotel rating: 4★+
Rooms: 27
Suites: 2
Single: 200–438€
Double: 200–438€
Breakfast: 23€
A one-star restaurant and an acclaimed hotel: the epitome of Provençal luxury.

La Bastide de Gordes & Spa

Chef: Olivier Bouzon
in the village
04 90 72 12 12
bastide-de-gordes.com
GaultMillau: ♨♨
Menu: 60/88€
À la carte: 90–150€
Hotel rating: 5★+
Rooms: 34
Suites: 7
Single: 137–405€
Double: 172–455€
Breakfast: 27€
This sumptuous hotel is right in the centre of Gordes. Make sure you get a room with a view: it will stay with you all your life.

RESTAURANT

Le Mas Tourteron

Chef: Elisabeth Bourgeois
chemin de Saint-Blaise, 4 km on the D2
04 90 72 04 90
mastourteron.com
GaultMillau: ♟♟
Menu: 55€
There are too few celebrated female chefs in France: here is one. Elisabeth Bourgeois specializes in the flavours of the South of France with a delicate Japanese touch.

HOTEL

Le Gordos

1.5 km along route de Cavaillon
04 90 72 00 75
hotel-le-gordos.com
Rating: 3★
Rooms: 19
Single: 121–169€
Double: 121–222€
Breakfast: 16€
At the entrance to Gordes (quieter than being in the midst of the central buzz), this is a gorgeous hotel with pool—essential in the summer months.

LUXURY RESTAURANT-HOTELS (NEARBY)

Restaurant Xavier Mathieu

Chef: Xavier Mathieu
Hostellerie Le Phébus & Spa
Joucas, 6.5 km on D102, then route de Murs
04 90 05 78 83
lephebus.com
Michelin:★
GaultMillau: ♟♟♟
Menu: 130€
À la carte: 75–140€
Hotel rating: 4★+
Rooms: 14

Suites: 10
Single: 200–320€
Double: 200–320€
Breakfast: 25€
A magnificent hotel on the plains below Gordes, this is a dream retreat with a Michelin-starred restaurant that highlights Provençal cuisine.

Le Mas de Herbes Blanches

Chef: Akhara Chay
Joucas, 6.5 km on D102, then route de Murs
04 90 05 79 79
herbesblanches.com
GaultMillau: ♟♟♟
Menu: 39 (weekday lunch)/90€
À la carte: 79–105€
Hotel rating: 4★
Rooms: 17
Suites: 2
Single: 150–600€
Double: 150–600€
Breakfast: 23€
There are stunning views across the Luberon at this luxury hotel with a highly rated restaurant run by Akhara Chay, a Frenchman of Cambodian and Thai heritage.

HOTEL (NEARBY)

Le Mas du Loriot

Joucas, 6.5 km on D102, then 4 km on route de Murs
04 90 72 62 62
masduloriot.com
Rating: 2★
Rooms: 7
Single: 105–145€
Double: 105–145€
Breakfast: 13€
An exquisite family-run hotel, with pool. Stay here and you'll wonder why the rich always go to five-stars.

GOULT

Goult is perched on a hill in the middle of the valley of the Luberon. With beautifully preserved and photogenic little streets, it has a nice feel, but lacks the magic I feel in towns like Bonnieux and Lourmarin. Let's say it is my least favourite of the local villages, but I still like it.

Being more populated with permanent residents than all the other villages may have something to do with it. The local people I encountered are all lovely and friendly, and will stop for a chat—for the first time, anyway. After having had one conversation with me in 'bastard French', they seem to cross the street very quickly when next spotting me from a distance! But it's their home and I feel like I shouldn't be intruding.

The village is well worth stopping at for an hour or so while driving through the area. It is the easiest of the villages to reach, as it's only a few minutes' drive off the highway.

The Café de la Poste is a great little bistro that serves a limited array of dishes and good local wines by the glass. Sit outside facing the square at dusk for a special way to see life go by.

RESTAURANTS

La Bartavelle
Chef: Gérard Lefèvre
rue de Cheval-Blanc
04 90 72 33 72
bartavelle.free.fr
Menu: 40€
An Art Déco gem with bistro food to match from the irrepressible Gérard Lefèvre (ex Lucas Carton and Lasserre).

Café de la Poste
rue République
04 90 72 23 23
À la carte: 17–35€
A picture-perfect Provençal bistro.

LACOSTE

This is probably the most beautiful of all the villages to look at from a distance. It is full of history, but does it have great food? Well, no, even though the sports bar has a great local atmosphere and the café has amazing views back over the valley.

Sit there and have a coffee in the early morning and get a glimpse of the sunrise, or go late in the afternoon when the light is perfect to pick up the layers of colour in the fields. It is very peaceful.

Lacoste is perhaps most famous for its association with the Marquis de Sade. He was an unusual aristocrat, a free-spirited and controversial philosopher and author, who inherited his uncle's château and lived there in the 1770s.

Today, the château is in a state of partial ruin. It has been under renovation since the end of World War II, but in the past 15 years Pierre Cardin has lovingly restored much of Lacoste to the point of reinvention. He has made the rest of France realize what a jewel the Petit Luberon is for its architecture, art and music.

Cardin also presides over the Festival de Lacoste in July and August. It is a series of musical, theatrical and other artistic events, including opera in the theatre formed in the quarry at the base of the village.

I do hope, though, that good food finds it way into this village soon, as it is the only thing missing here.

LOURMARIN

Lourmarin's market on Fridays is a great excuse to drive through the Grand Luberon to this pretty village. (Reine Sammut's restaurant is another!) We came along the ancient route from Bonnieux. It barely has the width to hold a campervan, let alone two coming at each other in both directions, followed by a petrol tanker and a couple of cyclists. Being in a dangerous place at the right time gives me a false sense of security and a feeling of belonging to the 'it's great to be alive' community of the Luberon.

Lourmarin is a beautiful, well-planned, old-world village with a grand château, housing the best wine *cave* in the area at the base of the château's front walls. A variety of second-hand bookstores also have their appeal, especially for old cookbooks. The three local pâtisseries are world class, and so is the antique and home-wares shop. The south-east side of the village has some stunning laneways full of great little cafés and restaurants dotted amongst the village's terraced houses.

RESTAURANT-HOTEL

La Fenière
Chef: Reine Sammut
Auberge La Fenière
2 km along rue de Cadenet
04 90 68 11 79
reinesammut.com
Michelin: ★
GaultMillau: ♟♟♟
Menu: 65/120€
À la carte: 100–134€
Hotel rating: 3★
Rooms: 16
Single: 150–320€
Double: 180–350€
Breakfast: included in room rate
The finest restaurant for miles and a hotel you will never want to leave. Chef Reine Sammut is the queen of the Luberon.

LUXURY HOTELS

Le Galinier de Lourmarin
in the village
04 90 75 98 52
bastidedugalinier.com
Rating: 5★
Week (Le Loft Rouge): 800–1200€
Week (La Maison du Chef): 2000–3400€
Week (La Vieille Bastide):
10~000–15~000€
Week (entire domaine): 12~000–20~00€

The Lourmarin property of Edouard Loubet, master chef and hotelier of La Bastide de Capelongue in Bonnieux. Perfection.

Le Moulin de Lourmarin
rue de Temple
04 90 68 06 69
moulindelourmarin.com
Rating: 4★
Rooms: 18
Suites: 2
Single: 110–340€
Double: 110–340€
Breakfast: included in room rate
Once a former 18th-century mill, it is now a welcoming and calm retreat.

HOTEL

Mas de Guilles
2 km on rue Vaugines
04 90 68 30 55
guilles.com
Rating: 3★
Rooms: 28
Single: 76–90€
Double: 76–230€
Breakfast: 15€
Nestled in 3 hectares of verdant garden and countryside, this is an enchanting home away from home.

RESTAURANT (NEARBY)

La Petite Maison de Cucuron
Chef: Eric Sapet
place de l'Étang, Cucuron, 7.5 km on D58
04 90 68 21 99
lapetitemaisondecucuron.com
Michelin: ★
GaultMillau: 👨‍🍳👨‍🍳
Menu: 40/60€
Fabulous and fresh Provençal cuisine.

HOTEL (NEARBY)

Le Pavillon de Galon
chemin de Galon, Cucuron, 7.5 km on D58
04 90 77 24 15
pavillondegalon.com
Rating: B&B+
Rooms: 3
Single: 175–240€
Double: 175–240€
Breakfast: included in room rate
This is listed as a bed-and-breakfast, but it is
a truly delightful and luxurious place to stay.

MÉNERBES

Ménerbes was made famous by Peter Mayle's *A Year in Provence*. But it is far more than just that. Ménerbes is the most liveable of the villages. It has everything an expat needs to satisfy the mind and remind one what it is like to live in Old Provence.

It has nowhere near as many tourists as you might think and the ones that do visit seem to be on some specific pilgrimage—some maybe for a glimpse of where photographer-poet Dora Mar once lived, others to capture the feel of the Peter Mayle experience, or still more to celebrate the medieval feel of the town and the purposeful lack of development that surrounds it.

The local vineyards and olive groves make this town very special. It doesn't have its own special bakery or a brilliant restaurant, and even the Friday market is very small, but it sells great tomatoes.

HOTEL-RESTAURANT

La Bastide de Marie
route de Bonnieux
04 90 72 30 20
labastidedemarie.com
Menu (dinner): 89€ (including wine)
À la carte (lunch): 34–64€
Hotel rating: 3★+
Rooms: 10
Suites: 5
Single: 220–350€
Double: 220–350€
Breakfast: 20€
In a village once famous for its almost perverse lack of hotels and restaurants (where did all those British tourists stay, *A Year in Provence* tightly gripped in their hands?), here is a Luberon gem. With views, gardens, and an elegant and romantic restaurant, what more could you want?

HOTEL-RESTAURANT (NEARBY)

La Bastide de Soubeyras
3 km on route des Beaumettes
04 90 72 30 20
bastidesoubeyras.com
Menu: 35€ including wine
Rating: B&B+
Rooms: 5
Single: 95–165€
Double: 95–165€
Breakfast: included in room rate
Situated in the Luberon National Park, this is a delightful place to stay, with a garden, pool and noted restaurant.

OPPÈDE-LE-VIEUX

Oppède-le-Vieux, which appears to cling to the side of a cliff, is a magnificent village. Built high on a rocky outcrop and surrounded by lush vegetation, the thick forests and rocks form a striking backdrop.

When visiting Oppède-le-Vieux in peak season, leave your car in the car park at the base of the village, which is signposted as the Botanical Gardens.

The Gardens are actually worth a stroll to look at juniper trees as well as the old wild cedars, before following the picturesque path up the hill. It is a steep walk, but well worth it.

During non-peak times, there is a small car park adjacent to the town square, but it fills well before 10 am.

This historic village was once a Roman garrison, but now is an empty relic with a couple of okay cafés. The one on the corner is not my favourite.

Don't be confused with the second part of the town, named Oppède, which is five minutes' drive at the base of the hill on which the ancient village sits. There is not much attraction in Oppède itself.

HOTEL (NEARBY)

La Bastide du Bois Bréant
501 chemin du Puits de Grandaou, Maubec,
6 km on route du Pont-Neuf
04 90 05 86 78
hotel-bastide-bois-breant.com
Rating: 3★
Rooms: 12
Suite: 1
Single: 128–220€
Double: 128–220€
Breakfast: included in room rate
Provençal, elegant and whisper-quiet.
The best rooms are delightful.

ROUSSILLON

This village was once a well-known place for artists to frequent. I say 'was' because Roussillon is now a tourist trap. Some of the tourist offerings in the shops are high quality, but most are not.

My heart is torn here as I really love this village, but I also hate the tourist hordes on big buses and the drop-off trucks for rented bikes. I would not like to be here in mid-summer.

Many of the restaurants follow the tourist path unfortunately, but I do recommend an early morning coffee or beer at the top of the village opposite the Hotel de Ville. If you are lucky, the Luberon's version of Smoky Dawson will be belting out a few slow tunes from his amplified guitar. I was nearly going to buy his CD that was on offer, but Phoenix loved his music and this may have just tipped me over the edge when I got back in Oz.

The market is every Thursday. Nothing overly impressive, but the produce is mainly local. A good cheese stand is worth the journey, as is the bakery.

RESTAURANT-HOTEL

Restaurant David

Chef: Jean Luc Laborie
Le Clos de la Glycine
place de la Poste
04 90 05 60 13
luberon-hotel.fr
GaultMillau: 😋😋
Menu: 55€
À la carte: 35–55€
Hotel rating: 3★+
Rooms: 9
Suite: 1
Single: 105–175€
Double: 105–175€
Breakfast: 13€
With glorious views from a dinning room that pays homage to Jean Luc Laborie's cuisine, this is an excellent restaurant-hotel.

HOTEL

Les Sables d'Ocre

route d'Apt
04 90 05 55 55
sablesdocre.com
Rating: 3★
Rooms: 22
Single: 65–88€
Double: 65–88€
Breakfast: 10€
It may be a modern take on traditional
Provençal architecture, but this
a genuine Luberon experience at
a very reasonable cost.

RESTAURANT-HOTEL (NEARBY)

Le Gourmet

Chef: Christophe Renaud
Domaine de la Coquillade
Gargas, 7.5 km on the D104, D4,
D83 and D1010
04 90 74 71 71
coquillade.fr
Michelin: ★
GaultMillau: 😋😋
Menu: 38 (weekday lunch)/49/57/75€
Hotel rating: 5★+
Rooms: 14
Suites: 14
Single: 150–360€
Double: 150–360€
Breakfast: 20€
A Michelin-starred restaurant in a stunning vaulted dining room, with a gorgeous and luxurious hotel attached. This is Luberon heaven.

WINES OF THE REGION

With wine more popular than bread and water in this part of the world, the most likely way to communicate with a French person is to have a glass of *vin* together. Not drinking wine with a meal can lead to ostracization from the French community.

If you drive 20 minutes east of Avignon, every backyard has access to a vineyard, and winemaking equipment fills nearly every garage. Wine is produced for the most part on very flat land and very cheaply. At certain times of the year its open-market price would be cheaper than the water that feeds the vines.

Unlike in most other countries, in Provence wine is considered a standard part of every lunch, with breakfast debatable. Having worked in this part of the world as a chef, I can vouch for regularly taking a glass of good rustic plonk with lunch. It's never abused; it's just there to make you appreciate your day.

The best way to describe the local appellations of the Luberon and Vaucluse (Southern Rhône) is that they are neither expensive nor reserved for special occasions. With everyday meals, basic local wines (*vins des pays*) are served.

On special occasions, there are a few well-established vineyards that are producing well-crafted, world-class wines. I list several below, although in this part of the world the style of wine does not necessarily match the quality of food. In the past decade, however, some young and exciting winemakers have emerged.

Provence covers eight major appellations, led by the Provence flagship, Bandol. I know Bandol well from selling its wines through my restaurants. Its heavy reds make a great match with the black winter truffle.

In my opinion, Bandol reds need a good ten years before consuming, which I learnt through conversations and the occasional tasting with legendary Melbourne chef Jacques Reymond, who shared his knowledge on the tradition of Bandol and truffles. The rich truffle, blackberry and red current flavours are built on a foundation of earthiness that very few other wines aim to produce.

Other Provence wines can be compared to the Southern Rhône wines as they share various grapes and, to some degree, style and climate. Provence also has a classification of its most prestigious estates, much like Bordeaux does.

CÔTES-DU-LUBERON

The Luberon is perhaps the most seasonal wine region of France and produces mostly table wines that are to be drunk *en primeur*, meaning the year they are produced. In other words, they are great quaffing wine, with the best results mainly rosé and red.

Vins de primeur (or nouveaux wines) are permitted by Appellation d'Origine Contrôlée (AOC) regulations to be sold in the same year that they are harvested. As of 2005, there were 55 such AOCs in France. Less than half are required to have the words 'en primeur' or 'nouveau' printed on the label. Depending on the AOC regulations, a nouveau wine may be red, rosé or white.

Red and rosé wines are made from Grenache, Syrah, Cinsault, Mourvèdre and Carignan (each to a maximum of 30%). Other varieties may be used to a maximum of 20%. These reds are distinctly characterized by their aromas of black fruit, spice and pepper.

White wines are produced from Clairette, Bourboulenc, Grenache Blanc and Roussanne (maximum 30%).

The appellation that best defines this en primeur style is the Côtes-du-Luberon. It spreads along the spine of hills that divide the Durance and Coulon rivers from L'Isle-sur-la-Sorgue through to Apt, sweeping through communes such as Oppède, Ménerbes, Lacoste, Bonnieux and Lourmarin.

The Côtes-du-Luberon appellation sits beside Côtes-du-Rhône and below Côtes-du-Ventoux (roughly separated by the road that runs from L'Isle-sur-la-Sorgue to Apt). It is a relatively recent appellation (1988). However, there is very serious money moving into the area and the wines here are causing some excitement in wine circles.

The style of wine depends on whether it is produced on the north-facing slopes looking towards Mont Ventoux or the south-facing slopes looking towards the Durance River, which marks its southern-most extent.

Most of the wines are either red or rosé. However, some of the whites are causing serious wine drinkers to sit up and take notice (for example, Château la Canorgue).

Below are some domain wines I have tasted that I would recommend. Being so close to the Southern Rhône, I really think for the 'special bottle' you need to look closely at these appellations. They are more expensive but well worth it.

I have asked a good mate, Julian Castagna of Castagna Vineyard near Beechworth, to help recommend some great wines of the region.

CÔTES-DU-LUBERON

Château la Canorgue
route de Pont-Julien
84480 Bonnieux
04 90 77 81 01
chateaucanorgue@vinsdusiecle.com

Domaine de la Cavale
route de Lourmarin
84160 Cucuron
04 90 72 22 96
domaine-la-cavale.com

M. Chapoutier
18 avenue du Docteur
26600 Tain-l'Hermitage
04 75 08 28 65
chapoutier.com

CÔTES-DU-VENTOUX

Domaine de Fondrèche
84380 Mazan
fondreche.com

Domaine du Tix
84570 Mormoiron en Ventoux
04 90 61 84 43
domaine-du-trix.com

Domaine Vindemio
34 avenue Jean Jaurès
84570 Villes-sur-Auzon
04 90 70 20 45
vinemio.com

PROVENCE

Domaine les Fouques
1405 route des Borrels
83400 Hyères
04 94 65 68 19
fouques-bio.com
Contact: Yves Gros

Château de Roquefort
13830 Roquefort la Bédoule
04 42 73 20 84
deroquefort.com
Contact: Raimond de Villeneuve

Château Romanin
13210 Saint-Rémy de Provence
04 90 92 45 87
romanin.com
Contact: Pascal Fraychet

Domaine Hauvette
La Haute Galine
13210 Saint-Rémy de Provence
04 90 92 03 90
domainehauvette@wanadoo.fr
Contact: Dominique Hauvette

Domaine de Trevallon
13103 Saint-Étienne-du-Gres
04 90 49 06 00
domainedetrevallon.com
Contact: Eloi Dürrbach

Château Ste Anne
Sainte-Anne-d'Evenos
83330 Evenos
04 94 90 35 40
chateaustanne@free.fr
Contact: Jean Baptiste Dutheil

Domaine Milan
13210 Saint-Rémy de Provence
04 90 92 12 52
dom-milan.com
Contact: Henri Milan

Domaine Sulauze
RN 569 Chemin du vieux Sulauze
13140 Miramas
04 90 58 02 02
domainedesalauze.com

Château Vignelaure
route de Jouques
83560 Rians
04 94 37 21 10
vignelaure.com

Château Simone
chemin de la Simone
13590 Meyreuil
04 42 66 92 58
chateau-simone.fr

RECIPES

≈≈≈

This book was designed and typeset by Trisha Garner.

The text was set in 9.5 point Meta Serif Book with
13 points of leading, and 9.5 point Meta Normal
with 12.5 points of leading.

The text is printed on 120 gsm woodfree.

This book was edited by Lucy Davison.